HORSE
FROM BASICS

Sovereign Books/New York

& RIDER
TO SHOW COMPETITION
JUDY RICHTER
with Photographs by SUE MAYNARD

For Lydia Frances Theurkauf

Published by Sovereign Books
A Simon & Schuster Division of
Gulf & Western Corporation
Simon & Schuster Building
1230 Avenue of the Americas
New York, New York 10020
Designed by Libra Graphics
Manufactured in the United States of America
10 9 8 7 6 5 4 3 2 1
Library of Congress Cataloging in Publication Data

Richter, Judy.
Horse and rider.

Bibliography: p.
Includes index.
SUMMARY: Discusses acquiring, training, and riding
a horse, and preparing for showing the horse in a show.
1. Show-riding. 2. Horse-shows. [1. Horses.
2. Horse shows. 3. Show riding] I. Maynard, Sue.
II. Title.
SF295.2.R48   798'.2   78-11735
ISBN 0-671-18369-9

"The rider is simultaneously
the teacher, instructor, trainer,
teammate, and leader"

Jean Saint-Fort Paillard

CONTENTS

FOREWORD

Judy Richter is not only a lovely person and a sincere horsewoman but also an old, old friend. I suppose we've known each other now through three decades, first as members of the "younger" horsey set, juniors in the 1950s. Our second acquaintance was in New York City. I was a fledgling (failing) actor at the Neighborhood Playhouse, and Judy was a newlywed, having just become Mrs. Max Richter. Janice Wylie, of the famed career-girls murder case and niece of author Philip Wylie, and I were acting partners and would often go to Judy's and Max's apartment to rehearse; they were both audience and critic. Soon I learned (thanks to Judy's honesty, which she is noted for) that Greek tragedy became a comedy and Restoration comedy became a tragedy through our particular efforts. My acting career, needless to say, soon fizzled.

Our riding relationship came about in the mid-1960s. She had a lovely German horse named Hyllis and I had a young student named Susan Bauer (now Mrs. Ronnie Mutch). We got horse and rider together, and they were quite a combination; I thought Judy and I a good team, as we thought so much alike even then. We also worked several jumpers together, and I was still at the stage of fat egg-butt snaffles and no martingales (true to real ostrich form). Judy took a little bit of the brunt of this era as the rider always being half-run off with. We both survived, and she soon developed into a more and more accomplished teacher and trainer.

Judy's forte as a teacher-trainer really stems from the fact that she understands and likes people as well as horses. She is a teacher of the individual and his personality. There is no feeling that one is lost in the shuffle or part of the crowd. She becomes sincerely involved in a student's problems and their solutions. Her stable atmosphere is always warm, positive, and full of fellowship, which is so important especially when working with youngsters. In short, she has everything going for her when one considers a good, all-round horsewoman.

I wish Judy luck in her grand endeavor to help people and further riding. Of course my main concern, personally, in the encouragement of good riding is for the benefit of the animal; concern for his well being should always be foremost. Educated riding is always the very first step towards fine training. Read this good book and you'll be well on your way to doing it right.

George H. Morris
Pittstown, New Jersey

PREFACE

This book is intended for riders who want to develop sound basics in hunt seat equitation and to school their horses well. The training methods that I use are mainly a combination of various techniques gleaned from other riders and trainers that I have tried myself and found helpful.

Some readers and riders may be baffled by the range of material covered here. You will find some fairly sophisticated concepts juxtaposed with simple, basic exercises. I do this for two reasons. First, I have found that many so-called advanced riders have never learned, for instance, to adjust their tack properly or to mount and to dismount correctly. Second, and more significantly, I have found that teaching intermediate and advanced riders together works very well, because the same principles apply regardless of the rider's level. The necessity of teaching nearly all my students during the waning daylight hours after school forced me to group together riders of different levels.

Combined classes have been successful because the exercise at hand is often a review for the advanced riders who in turn are able to demonstrate whatever point I am making to the intermediate riders. I teach to the top of the class, challenging the most able rider of the group and then modifying the exercise sufficiently so the less advanced riders are not overwhelmed. Once the intermediates have seen the advanced riders perform the task, they have a better notion of how they will go about it.

If you are a rider who, for geographical or other reasons, does not have the benefit of good daily supervision, you must make an effort to go where the action is. There are excellent clinics all over the country, so try to get to as many as possible. There you may meet someone who can help you with your riding, whether it is the person giving the clinic or another participant. Also, you should make an effort to spend a few days, a couple of weekends, or several weeks with a horseman or horsewoman you respect. All riders need someone to rely on for advice about their horses, their riding, and their whole program. I have several very talented riders in the Northwest whom I see several times a year and talk to on the phone occasionally. They make wonderful progress on their own, and it is always a pleasure to get together with them and see how they are developing.

All serious riders have to be good observers. Try to attend some of the major horse shows and watch the top riders—in the schooling area as well as in the ring. See what works and what does not, and try to figure out why. When my sister and I were in the junior division, we didn't have a trainer, so we used to watch Dave Kelley and try to ride like him. We learned a lot this way.

Your own horses are good teachers and they will indicate very clearly to you how good a training job you are doing. Sympathetic riders are flexible in their training methods because they understand what their horses are telling them.

The serious rider must also learn by being a serious reader. We are most fortunate that two of our most knowledgeable and articulate horsemen, George Morris and Bill Steinkraus, have written excellent books describing their philosophies and methods. Morris's *Hunter Seat Equitation* and Steinkraus's *Riding and Jumping* both bear reading and rereading. As your thinking about riding develops, you will bring more to them and gain more insight from them.

Taking classes, attending clinics, being a keen observer and a sympathetic rider—all these can help you become more skillful. To become a rider good enough to compete at the tops shows, what do you need? Sue Mutch, who runs a first-class show stable with her husband, answered that question most aptly: "You need at least two and preferably all three of the following: talent, interest, and family support."

We all can recognize talent, but defining it is not easy. All talented riders I know have a real rapport with their horses. Riders of hunters and jumpers who are blessed with a good eye for a distance to the jumps are light-years ahead of the rest of us who have to learn to find a distance. Talented riders also have what my assistant, Ellen Raidt, calls good body control. You simply tell them what to do and they do it.

Interest is perhaps the most important quality to look for in a good rider. The interested youngster who hangs around the stable, mucking stalls and cleaning tack, is the one who is going to get the extra rides when it is too cold or too rainy for the fair-weather riders.

Support means financial *and* moral support: both are essential. It is expensive to buy, train, and show a good horse at the top shows; even keeping a plain old horse in your backyard is not cheap. I know many families who make sacrifices so that one or more of their children can keep a horse and ride. The endless feed bills, blacksmith bills, vet bills, and entry fees—not to mention the necessary clothes and saddlery—are very hard on the pocketbook.

But, more important than financial support is moral support and encouragement. I have always been very fortunate in this regard. My parents, Philip and Mary Hofmann, were up countless mornings before sunrise to help me get ready for whatever I was to face: the show, hunt, dressage test, three-day event, point to point. They were careful not to offer advice unless I asked for it, which I probably should have done more often. I am still blessed with lots of family support. My husband Max and my children, Hans and Philip, give me encouragement. Believe me, it makes all the difference.

1

Finding the Right Horse

"Can I—should I—buy a horse?" Almost everyone who is serious about riding asks that question sooner or later.

To decide in your own case, first assess your level of riding ability. I think it is unwise to buy a horse until you have reached the low intermediate level. At this stage, a rider is able to walk, trot, and canter. Further, the low intermediate knows how to post on the proper diagonal and put the horse on the proper lead at the canter.

Until this stage is reached, a rider is better off riding safe, reliable school horses in a structured lesson situation. Rapid progress is possible under the supervision of a teacher, and the novice is less likely to get into dangerous, frightening situations than he would be in trying to cope with a horse of his own.

Learning to ride at the low intermediate level takes quite a lot of practice and perseverance. But even more time and dedication is re-

SUE MAYNARD

Max Richter holding Johnny's Pocket. This horse has a lovely expression—intelligent, alert, and calm.

quired of people who own their own horses. Riding and training the horse are just the beginning of your responsibilities. You will have to find a good place to keep him, whether in your own back yard, at a friend's place, or at a public boarding stable. And there are expenses to be met for feed, veterinarians' fees, and shoeing. A horse needs to be shod every four to six weeks. He needs to be wormed often, and he should have annual immunizations against a variety of equine diseases.

Buying a horse is not at all like buying an item of sports equipment. It's true, horses do come in a variety of sizes and price ranges, as do skis, tennis rackets, and ice skates. But there the resemblance ends. Each horse is an individual with its very own qualities. And since this is true of people too, it is essential to make a good match between horse and rider. The same horse might be perfect for one person and disastrous for somebody else.

You are ready to buy a horse, if you have reached the low intermediate stage and are prepared to devote the necessary time to riding and looking after a horse. Next consult someone who is a professional in the horse business for help in selecting the best horse available. Start with your own riding teacher. Most people who teach have some knowledge of the horses being offered for sale locally, and your own teacher is familiar with your specific needs and tastes. For their work in locating good, sound prospects, most professionals charge the buyer 10 percent of the purchase price, and that is usually money well spent. A professional knows how to recognize the flaws beneath a pretty color or a shiny coat.

Regardless of your level of riding ability, I think it is important to ride the horse several times before buying it or dismissing it as a possibility. This will show whether the horse and rider are compatible. Novice riders tend to be nervous and tense the first time on a strange horse. Usually it will be better the next day, especially if all went well the first time.

If you are out of touch with local horse activity, then you will have to make an effort to find a good professional. Attend some nearby clinics or horse shows, if possible, and watch the trainers you see there. If you admire the way a trainer handles his riders and horses, approach him and explain what you want. If you have no luck with this method, write to the American Horse Shows Association, 598 Madison Avenue, New York, NY 10022, and ask the association to recommend a reliable trainer in your area. The AHSA is a national organization and usually can suggest a number of people in even the most remote areas who are qualified to advise prospective buyers.

Once you have found someone to help you select a horse, give him or her some time—say, a month or so—to come up with some likely candidates. Finding suitable horses is not easy, since they have to be looked over carefully. If a professional doesn't come up with a horse right away, don't assume he is not trying. If an ad catches your eye, let your adviser follow it up rather than doing so yourself. He may know the horse already and consider it unsuitable; in any case, he is better able than you are to ask the right questions about the horse and the people who are selling it. Certainly, don't put him on the spot by trying the horse yourself and *then* asking his opinion.

The most important considerations in evaluating a horse are the following: temperament, size and suitability, age and experience, ability or talent, and soundness.

The temperament of a rider's first horse is particularly important. In fact, the more I work with horses, the more value I place on good disposition, no matter what kind of job I want the horse to do. A horse should be generous, pleasant, and willing. He should not be cranky or stubborn, or hot and quick. Difficult, high-strung, spoiled, even roguey horses make interesting projects for able, experienced, and talented riders, but most horsemen agree that a horse with temperament problems is likely to let you down just when you need him most, whether it be your first Maclay class or the Olympic games.

Even if you know very little about horses, you can discern up to a point whether a horse has a good temperament or not. Watch the groom or owner catch him in his stall or paddock. Watch him being brushed off and saddled up. Does he stand quietly in the cross ties, or does he fret or bite and kick when being worked on? Some horses have bad stable manners, even though they are pleasant to ride. Leave them for the experienced riders and trainers, especially if you plan to keep your horse at home and care for him yourself.

Watch him being mounted. Does he stand obediently, or does he prance off when the rider is halfway up? While being ridden, is he pleasantly compliant, or is he keen and hard to control? Or sluggish and balky?

As with people, horses' eyes tell a lot about their personalities. A big, kind eye is a good sign. Beware of the horse with a white ring around his eye. Nine times out of ten, such a horse will prove to be evasive and unreliable, at worst, a rogue. Beware also of the startled eye. That horse is probably nervous and high-strung.

Horses' ears are expressive, too. A horse that pricks his ears and looks cheerful about his work is a good bet. Not so the horse that habitually pins his ears back against his head; he does not enjoy what he is doing. He may simply be cranky by nature, or, as is often the

OPPOSITE: *Philip Richter age seven on his Frosty Lad, a wonderful first pony. During the summer he is quiet as an old cow since he is turned out all day every day; when it is cold, he needs 15 to 20 minutes on the longe line before he is foolproof for a young rider. He is a good jumper and can bring along his rider from the short stirrup stage up through the pony hunter division. He is not fancy but he is good, and even at the best horse shows he will not be out of place.*

case, he may be uncomfortable, unsound in some way. Whatever the reason, you do not want a horse that has a sour expression.

A second important consideration when selecting your horse is his size and suitability. If he is much too big for you, you will have all sorts of difficulties, beginning with such mundane matters as grooming and tacking him up. More serious problems may develop later in your riding. A small rider, for example, may be unable to follow the stride and jumping arc of a large horse. On the other hand, you don't want to buy a horse that you will outgrow very soon. Large riders on small horses have an even worse time. We see large children showing their too small ponies with less and less success as they struggle to keep the upper body and legs in the right places. Remember, also, a horse's size includes more than just his height. There are big-little horses and there are little-big horses. What matters is the specific rider on the specific horse, not whether the horse is 15.3 hands or 16.1 hands high: a short-legged, long-waisted rider needs a tall, narrow horse; a very long-legged rider, a big barreled horse that will fill out his leg.

Suitability also means that horse and rider have to be comfortable with each other. A rider who is passive by nature is likely to get along better with a more aggressive horse. A timid rider, on the other hand, may be frightened by an aggressive horse and feel more at ease on a placid horse of the sort that has to be pushed along. Very aggressive riders are likely to unsettle a sensitive, high-strung horse, so they need a more tolerant mount.

As a rule of thumb, buy the quieter horse. Presumably, if the seller knows what he is doing, you are seeing the horse at his best, so if he doesn't suit you now, he probably never will. In any case, rely heavily on your professional's advice as to suitability.

For a first horse, you definitely want something "made"—not a green horse—and something old rather than young. I wouldn't hesitate to buy a horse ten or twelve years old if he was just right in other respects. A more experienced rider may want to work with a young, green horse, but he should not undertake such a project unless he has a lot of help from a professional trainer. It is very easy to ruin young horses by expecting too much or too little from them. As to the sex of the horse, it has been my experience that geldings are usually more stable and reliable than mares, though of course there are always exceptions.

The next question to consider is the horse's talent and ability.

SUE MAYNARD

Best Be Bold owned by Sophia Estrada. This little horse is the kind a novice buyer would be apt to overlook in favor of a shinier model with a white blaze and white legs. When we bought him early in November, he was a thin, nondescript mousebrown. He was quite a good mover on the flat and a very good jumper so we bought him. He was already improving by the time this picture was taken and by spring he was a very cute horse.

Here again, you must rely on your professional's expertise. I think a child's first horse should be able to negotiate courses in the maiden, novice, limit equitation, and children's hunter levels, up to the Medal and Maclay Equitation classes. Such a horse should be capable of jumping a 3-foot 6-inch equitation course and should have a stride long enough to cover the distances. A 12-foot stride, at least, is necessary for the average equitation course today.

When you go to look at the horse, the seller should be able to demonstrate that the horse can indeed perform to the level you hope to reach eventually. It is important to see for yourself that the horse is capable; don't just take someone's word that he can do it. (I remember going with my sister years ago to try Salem, who later became a famous international jumper. Dave Kelley, who was then and still is one of the most highly regarded, professional horsemen in the country, had the horse at that time. After Carol jumped the course that Dave had set up, he said, "Well, some day, girl, you may want him to jump six feet. Let's see if he can." So Dave set up a huge six-foot jump, my sister turned white, and Salem sailed over it with ease.)

When buying green horses, you obviously cannot ask them for such demonstrations of their ability, but with experience you will learn to judge them from seeing how they do simple things. Make a simple cross-rail gymnastic, for instance, and watch especially how the horse bends his knees and rounds his back. In the meantime, rely

Carol Hofmann Thompson on Salem.

on someone "with a good eye for a horse," especially if you are considering a young, green horse.

Like Salem, most of our best show hunters and jumpers are Thoroughbred horses, many with histories on the race track. Although some of them have famous jumping bloodlines, this I think is less important than the individuality of the horse. I would not pass over what I thought was a good horse just because he was not a pure Thoroughbred. Indeed, Thoroughbreds tend to be a little too keen to make good first horses; for this, a half-bred Quarter Horse may be the better choice. It really does not matter how a horse is bred if he suits you and you like him.

Finally there is the question of soundness. You have to expect an older horse to show a certain amount of wear and tear. To some extent you can live with soundness problems. Corrective shoeing can be helpful in some cases and, for showing, the anti-inflammatory drug Butazolidin will give some relief from arthritis and other old-age difficulties. However, I think it is poor judgment to buy a young horse with soundness problems, because the problems surely will worsen as the horse ages. The time you spend training him could be wasted if he is eventually too unsound to do his job. Have a veterinarian examine your proposed purchase; he should X-ray the horse's feet and anything else he thinks necessary.

Be sure to tell the veterinarian how you intend to use the horse. Without this knowledge he can't advise you correctly on whether to buy or not. For instance, a horse that may not be up to competing in world-class three-day events could last for years as an equitation horse. Similarly, a horse that is not equal to showing two divisions every weekend might be a good buy for someone who wants to ride a couple of times a week and show occasionally.

Finally, if the veterinarian says buy him, and the professional says buy him, then buy him and get on with it.

Now that you have bought your wonderful new horse, you have a lot of new responsibilities. You have to make sure that he has the very best care and proper training as well. Every rider, regardless of whether he works mostly on his own or has a competent trainer at his elbow every minute, is responsible for the training of his horse. As George Morris so aptly puts it in his excellent book, *Hunter Seat Equitation:*

> Horses get better or worse according to who is riding them. They
> do not maintain levels on their own, and vacillation, indecision, and

ignorance create mediocre or poor riding and bad horses. The rider who goes for an hour's work knowing how to improve his form, aware of the correct aid application, coordination, and sequence for various results, and who has a variety of schooling exercises at his fingertips—this rider does things well. He will enjoy hacking through the country, he will fox hunt with the best, compete favorably in the showing, be able to school and develop his own winners. From every point of view, a comprehensive understanding of the sport has its rewards, whether safety, performance, or both. (page 98)

2

Equipment

The Schooling Ring

If you ride at a large boarding stable, you probably will have the use of the ring and a wide array of jumps. However, if you keep your horse at home, you will need to set up a schooling area with the proper kind of footing and a variety of jumps.

Your schooling area should be rectangular and fairly flat. A fence enclosing it is useful but is not absolutely necessary. I think a home ring should have dressage letters properly in place. They serve as focal points and encourage accuracy on the part of horse and rider. (For placement of letters, see the diagrams in chapter 5.)

It is important from the standpoint of soundness to maintain good footing in the area where you school your horse. The feet, legs, and

Cavalletti set 3 to 4 feet apart for trotting. The X-standards holding the cavalletti in the picture above keep them from moving when hit. In the picture below, the rails are set in notched holders, like that in the close-up (made from a broken jump rail).

back of the horse simply cannot take a lot of pounding on hard ground. To appreciate the effect this has on a horse, try walking for a couple of miles on hard pavement. Your feet, legs, and back will begin to ache from the repeated shocks to the muscles and joints. While there is not much we can do about the hard ground so often encountered at horse shows, especially during the summer months, at least we can provide the best possible footing for our horses at home.

The ground of your schooling area should have good drainage. Sometimes runoff can be improved by a few well-placed shallow ditches. Excellent footing can be achieved by spreading a layer of "dead sand" to a depth of about six inches. This is a mixture of sand and dirt that you can buy from a building or paving contractor. Dead sand drains well and stays soft in almost all weather conditions. We

TOP: *Cavalletti set 11 feet apart as a no-stride gymnastic.* BOTTOM: *A small oxer made of cavalletti.*

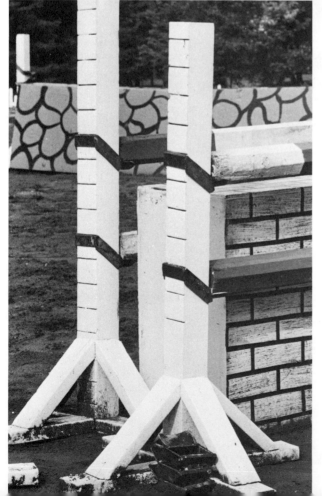

TOP: *Wing standards with cups and pins. Such equipment is commonly used at horse shows. The narrow gate is a recycled paddock gate.* BOTTOM: *Typical single pole 4-by-4-inch standards. The jump cups slide over the top of the standard and fit into the grooves on the back. These particular standards have lasted fifteen years, mostly because they have not been weakened by holes drilled for the more common cups with pins.*

oil our ring once every two or three years with used crank case oil to keep the dust down and prevent freezing during the winter. Your gas station should be able to suggest a source for the used oil.

A set of jumps is essential to your schooling program. A simple but expensive way to acquire jumps is to order a complete set from a company that specializes in building them. However, you can sometimes get professionally built jumps for less money by buying them second-hand after they have been used at a horse show.

Building your own standards and cavalletti is not difficult if you have the right tools. The photographs here show a number of jumps that can be contrived from fairly simple materials. For schooling at home I prefer the 4-by-4-inch single-pole standard rather than the wing standards commonly used at horse shows. They are lighter and easier to move, and they take up less room in your ring, which is an advantage if you are working in a limited area.

In addition to the usual rail jumps, build some with fillers. Be inventive, so that your horse will not be surprised by the color and variety of the jumps he will encounter at shows. A junk yard is a

A barrel jump. With 9 to 12 barrels, you can make a jump of regular size.

good source for things to use, such as barrels and old tires. Barrels can be laid end-to-end or upright. My favorite barrel jump is a pyramid of nine barrels, six forming the base and three on top. Tires can be piled on the ground, leaned against a rail, or hung from a rail. An old tarpaulin can be used to simulate a liverpool or water jump. There are endless possibilities if you use your imagination, but take care to build safe jumps with nothing protruding that could cause injury to rider or horse in the event of a fall and be sure not to leave extra jump cups on the standards.

Clothes and Equipment

A young rider looks well turned out in jodhpurs and jodhpur boots or laced paddock boots. Buff and rust are the usual colors for jodhpurs. Both look well, though buff will show dirt sooner than rust. When you are past the pony and limit equitation divisions and are showing in open equitation, hunter, or jumper classes, it's time to wear breeches and boots. Ready-made stretch breeches usually fit well and last a long time if they are properly cared for.

Boots will probably be your most expensive item of clothing. For the best appearance and fit, I suggest you invest in a pair of custom-made boots, either black dress boots or laced brown field boots. In either case, have them made unlined, since they will be softer and hence more comfortable and will allow a better feel of the horse. They will prove their worth in the long run over ready-made boots, which usually are too stiff or too short or too wide in the leg.

You will look your best in neat, unobtrusive riding clothes. Of course, nothing fits quite so well as custom-made shirts and jackets, but most riders can get nearly the same effect by having a ready-made coat altered to fit. A plain navy blue or dark green coat with dark buttons is a good choice. (I personally don't care for the velvet collars that are currently in style.)

Girl's ratcatcher shirts or chokers should be in plain pastel colors or white. A choker or shirt collar must fit perfectly; anything large or baggy looks very sloppy indeed. Many girls now put their monograms on their chokers in colors that coordinate with their jackets— a nice touch. Boys, of course, should wear their conservative ties neatly tacked down, not flapping in the breeze.

In the matter of headgear, a black or navy blue hunt cap is correct for any occasion. Girls with long hair should keep it pinned up

Barbara Ann Pyfrom of Nassau, Bahamas, and Coker Farm's Freedom. Twiggy demonstrates proper attire for a Limit Equitation rider. Her jodhpurs, boots, and coat are ready-made but fit well. Her appearance is neat and most definitely appropriate for one-day horse shows.

securely under a hair net. Boys should keep their hair short enough for a neat appearance. Wear the absolute minimum of jewelry.

Gloves are a matter of taste; if you wear them, they should be dark brown. I think your hands have just as good a feel with gloves on as without them, and they give you a more polished look in equitation classes. In rainy weather they are essential, since without them the reins are very slippery.

Sarah Bull on Best Mistake. Polished and poised and waiting to go in the ring. Her attire is impeccable.

Whether to wear spurs depends on your expertise as a rider, on your horse's disposition, and on the situation at hand. If you wear spurs before you have achieved good control of your seat, hands, and lower leg, you will probably get into trouble, since an unintentional jab can turn the quietest plug into a runaway. Spurs are more often needed in hot weather than in cold, in small, spooky indoor rings than in open fields. Still, some horses are so sluggish that they need prodding, even in the biggest field on the coldest, windiest day. You must use your judgment on whether or not to wear spurs.

I prefer Prince of Wales spurs to the hammerhead type. To me, they look more graceful and elegant. They come in lengths from ½ inch to 1½ inches, so you can buy exactly the length that suits your needs.

A stick, I believe, is a necessary aid for every rider who is past the beginning stage. Almost any horse can learn to accept the stick, no matter how tense and nervous he may be, and by using it you can often prevent a serious situation from developing. Learn to carry the stick in either hand comfortably. In most cases, it should be used behind the saddle, but occasionally a tap on the shoulder is useful, as when a horse is about to bulge one way or the other. Sticks come in a variety of lengths. A 14-inch stick is about right; it is long enough to be effective but short enough to be held easily and out of the horse's range of vision.

Naturally, you can dress more informally when you are not showing. Chaps and paddock boots are comfortable for everyday riding and schooling sessions, especially if you have to work your riding

LEFT: *Spur correctly placed on the rider's boot.* RIGHT: *Spur set rather low where its effect will be less severe. A shorter spur placed higher on the boot would look neater and have the same effect. Some horses need less spur than others and if a rider has only one pair of spurs, setting them lower on the boot makes them less severe. Notice also the spur strap is hanging loose, not neatly tucked in as in the picture at the left.*

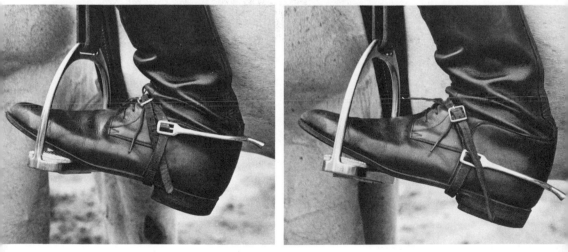

TOP: *The proper way to carry the stick.* CENTER: *Some riders prefer to carry the stick up along the arm, but I think it serves no purpose and distorts the position of the rider's hands.* BOTTOM: *Use of the stick behind the saddle.*

time in between other activities. Always ride in boots that have heels. If you wear flat shoes, such as sneakers, your foot can slide through the stirrup, and in the event of a fall you could be dragged fatally. (If any of my riders appears in flat shoes, he or she has to ride that day without stirrups.)

Also for safety's sake, wear a hunt cap whenever you ride, and be sure it fits snugly so that it stays put on your head.

Correct schooling attire for cold weather—chaps and paddock boots, heavy sweater, and down vest.

Here are some hints for cold-weather riding. If you buy sheepskin-lined boots, remember that they must be able to move freely in your stirrup irons. If they are too wide, you risk getting your foot caught in the iron, which can be dangerous. At winter shows you can wear a pair of rubbers with sheepskin or heavy felt innersoles over your regular riding boots for extra warmth. When taking a lesson in cold weather, don't wear something like a fat goosedown parka that prevents your instructor from seeing your upper body. Wear a vest or windbreaker under the parka so you can shed the latter after the first few minutes when you have warmed up.

Saddlery

Riders can choose from a wide variety of saddle designs. Some like overstuffed, deep-seated saddles, but I prefer a light, flat saddle without knee rolls or extra padding. This allows closer contact between you and the horse and gives you a better feel for what is going on under you. Saddle pads made of double-faced acrylic sheepskin are very attractive; they are also practical because they can be machine-washed. For a horse with a sensitive back, I recommend using a thick foam pad. I usually cut off the part of the foam that goes under the skirt of the saddle, so that there will not be too much bulk under the rider's leg. As for girths, I use those with elastic at one or both ends. They can be cinched up more tightly than the plain leather ones without causing discomfort to the horse. As a result, the saddle has less tendency to slide back.

The bridle I use in most situations is a snaffle bridle, usually a full-cheek snaffle held securely by leather bit loops. Intermediate and even advanced riders find it especially helpful in keeping a horse from bulging. It can be used with a variety of mouthpieces. As a general rule, I prefer thinner bits to thicker bits; the latter seem to invite horses to lug and lean. A smooth or slightly twisted mouthpiece works well in most cases. More severe versions, such as double or single twisted wire, are usually best left to riders above the intermediate level unless you are closely supervised by a professional. In the show ring, when fingertip control is necessary for smooth hunter performance, a sharper bit may be the correct choice. At home, however, you should school your horse in a plain snaffle and concentrate on making him more obedient.

Bridles made of leather ⅝ to ¾ of an inch wide show a horse's

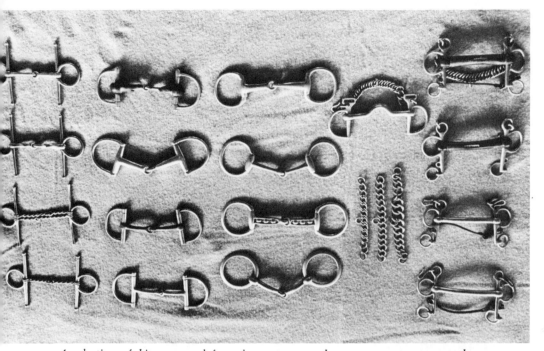

A selection of bits arranged from least severe at the top to most severe at the bottom. On the left are full-check snaffles (from top to bottom: plain, twisted, double-twisted-wire, single-twisted-wire). Next to them are D snaffles: The rubber coated snaffle at the top and the thick one below it are light on the mouth. The copper snaffle below them, like the rubber coated one, encourages the horse to chew the bit. The small D snaffle on the bottom is more severe. In the middle are three egg-butt snaffles, plus a loose-ring snaffle at the bottom. The roller-egg-butt bit above the loose-ring snaffle encourages chewing. The loose-ring snaffle is a good bit to use at home for daily flat work. On the far right are Pelham bits. The top two are vulcanized rubber. Like the Kimberwicke to their left, they are used with curb chains (the thicker the chain, the less severe). The "Tom Thumb" (shorter-shanked) Pelhams (top and third) are less severe than their longer-shanked counterparts.

head to better advantage than bridles of a wider leather. I also prefer reins in the same narrow widths. Thick reins feel clumsy to me, and I discourage their use, although some riders seem more comfortable with them.

It is a good practice for riders to use the standing martingale for showing over jumps until they are advanced enough to compete in classes under the sponsorship of the U.S.E.T. (United States Equestrian Team) or the F.E.I. (Fédération Equestre Internationale), in which standing martingales are prohibited.

The martingale prevents the horse from throwing his head up, even bumping the rider in the face, as he tries to evade the bit. When properly adjusted, the standing martingale affords the rider much more control without hampering the horse's use of his head and neck. In fact, some high-headed horses jump in better form when somewhat strongly restrained by a tight standing martingale. Ben O'Meara, one of the most talented jumper riders of all time, often used a very tight standing martingale with enormous success. On most horses, the standing martingale is correctly adjusted when there is just a slight slack in it while the horse is standing still with his head held normally.

Many purists claim that a well-schooled horse does not need a martingale. There is something to be said for that, but we are not all world-class riders, nor are our horses endowed with ideal conformation. Many, besides, do not start out with proper schooling. A standing martingale is a great help in steadying a green horse, and for the novice rider it provides a handy strap to hold on to in an emergency. Why not take advantage of this aid if it means winning a hunter class rather than losing just because the horse pushed up his nose for a fraction of a second on the far turn?

More advanced riders may want to experiment with the running martingale, which works on the bars of the horse's mouth rather than the corners. When it is properly adjusted, the running martingale should exert no tension on the reins; it comes into play only when the horse raises his head to evade the bit. I have not had much success in using running martingales on hunters and equitation horses. Some horses seem to resist more when they feel the pressure on the bars of the mouth. Although riders in international competition often use it successfully, for most riders the standing martingale is more helpful.

One final word about equipment. Don't settle for anything but the proper equipment and be sure that it is properly cared for. The book *A Horse of Your Own,* by M. A. Stoneridge, goes into these matters in great detail, and offers very sound guidance.

3

Getting Ready to Ride

Before mounting, go over all the tack to make sure it is adjusted properly. As rider it is your responsibility to do this every time you ride, even if you tacked up the horse yourself.

Make sure the bit is correctly positioned in the horse's mouth, neither too high nor too low. The noseband should be just below the cheekbone and should fit snugly. The martingale should be long enough to allow only a slight slack when the horse is standing normally. If there is a curb chain, see that it lies flat and is secured by a lip strap. Are all the straps on the bridle secure in their keepers? Flapping straps will annoy any horse, and once you are mounted it is awkward to try to secure them, especially if the horse is fresh or spooky.

Now examine the saddle, saddle pad, and girth. The pad should

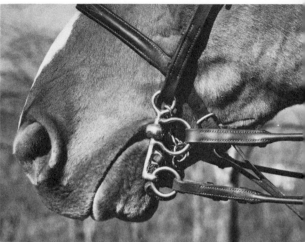

LEFT: *A bit holder for a full-cheek snaffle bit properly attached to the bridle.* RIGHT: *A steel pelham bit properly adjusted. A bit that hangs too low in a horse's mouth invites him to put his tongue over it, and serious mouth problems result.* BELOW: *Snaffle bridle and standing martingale properly adjusted.*

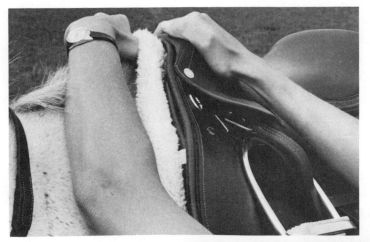

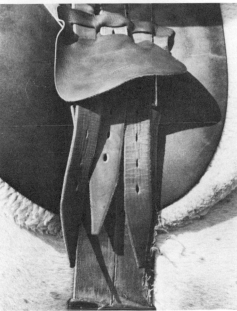

TOP: *Pulling the pad up into the pommel so it does not bind the horse's withers.* RIGHT: *Billet guard properly pulled down over the girth buckle. Notice that the elastic on the girth is frayed and should be replaced.*

be pulled up into the pommel of the saddle so that it does not bind the horse's withers. The loops for keeping the pad in place ought to be over the billet straps of the saddle. Do not pull the girth too tight at first. Many horses are what is termed "cinchy"—they tend to buck or bounce around if the girth is cinched up too sharply. Often a horse will defend himself against this treatment by "blowing up" and holding his breath. Before you mount, walk the horse a few steps and adjust the girth as necessary.

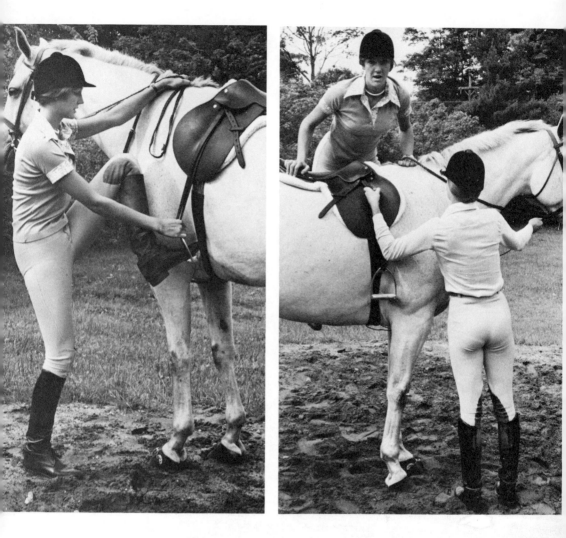

Mounting. ABOVE, LEFT: *The toe pressed against the girth not the horse's ribs.* RIGHT: *The groom or assistant should grasp the martingale, not the bit, with the hand holding the horse. Hold the stirrup leather as well to prevent the saddle from slipping.* OPPOSITE, LEFT: *Support your weight somewhat with the right hand on the front of the saddle. Put your right foot in the stirrup before you sink gently down into the saddle.* RIGHT: *Mounted and ready to ride.*

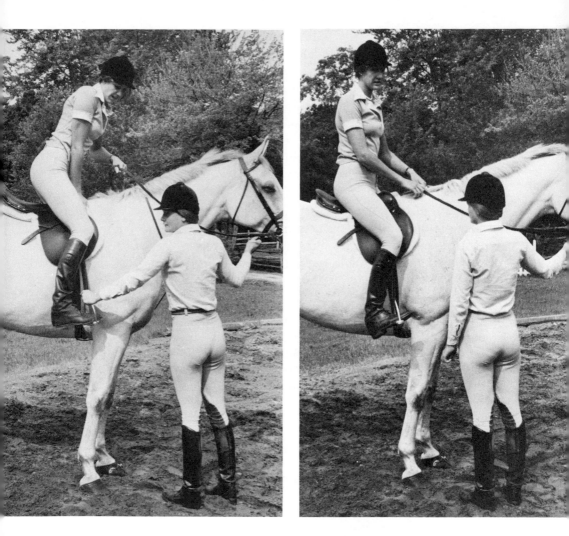

Mounting

The conventional and correct way of mounting is also the most efficient way; more important, it is the safest way. Standing on the horse's left side, take both reins in your left hand and rest that hand on the horse's mane just in front of the withers, grabbing a piece of mane if you must. Hold the reins evenly and with a fair degree of contact with the horse's mouth so that he does not move off; do not hold them so tight that he starts to move backwards, however. If he starts to turn toward you or away, adjust the reins accordingly.

Face toward the rear of the horse, so that once you have put your foot in the stirrup you will be in a position to swing up into the saddle, even if the horse should move off quickly. Use your right hand to steady the stirrup iron as you place your left toe into it, pressing the toe carefully against the girth. Don't stick your toe abruptly into the horse's ribs. If treated this way, even the most patient school horse cannot be blamed for moving off, leaving the rider to hop along after on one foot. Once the left foot is secure in the stirrup, with your right hand grasp the cantle of the saddle or better—if you can reach it—the skirt on the far side of the saddle. Now hoist yourself up, using the combined strength of your legs and arms. Once you are partway up, support yourself by moving your right hand to the far side of the pommel. Then slip your right foot into the stirrup and settle gently into the saddle.

Settling carefully into the saddle is very important for the horse's comfort and equanimity. A rider who flops onto his horse's back when mounting is certainly off to a bad start. My sister's Grand Prix horse Salem was particularly intolerant of clumsy mounting. He simply dumped you on the ground, an experience I happen to share with a world show jumping champion and several other victims. A good horseman shows consideration, even in the simple exercise of mounting. Insensitivity, on the other hand, is the mark

Proper way to shorten reins. Hold right rein with left hand, as shown, and slide right hand up toward horse's head. Then reverse the process: hold with the right and slide with the left.

of a mediocre rider and always prevents him or her from ever achieving real success.

Dismounting

There are two conventional methods for the dismount: sliding off and stepping off, also done on the left side of the horse. Each method requires that you take the reins in the left hand. In sliding off, drop both stirrups before swinging the right leg over the horse's rump and vaulting down. In stepping off, leave the left foot in its stirrup until you have swung your right leg over the horse's rump and have alighted on the ground.

Of the two methods, sliding off is by far the safer and more efficient method, since it does not involve the risk of being dragged if the horse shies or scoots away while the left foot is still in the stirrup.

Now that you have dismounted, immediately run both stirrup irons up the inside of the stirrup leather and tuck the remaining leather through the irons. Then the irons cannot flap against the horse's sides as he moves and frighten him.

Lead the horse with the reins drawn over his head; this gives you far better control than if the reins are left resting over the horse's neck.

Stirrup Adjustment

The length of the stirrup is set according both to the conformation of the horse and rider and to the kind of equestrian activity that is to be done.

Before you mount adjust the stirrup leathers to match your arm's length. Do this by placing your fingertips on the stirrup bar and lengthening the leather until the stirrup iron has touched the armpit of the straightened arm. Once you have mounted, check the correctness of the stirrup length and adjust it as necessary. At its proper length the iron should strike your ankle bone or just below it when your legs are stretched down. This length is usually most comfortable for riding cross-country or showing hunters. You may want your stirrups a little shorter if you are showing in the jumper division, or a little longer if you are working your horse on the flat or riding in hunt seat equitation flat class.

Dismounting. ABOVE: *Both feet out of the stirrups.* BELOW: *Slide down.*

After dismounting. The stirrup irons are run up and the reins are slipped over the horse's head so that you have better control when leading him to the stable.

On a fat, round horse who "takes up more leg," a slightly longer stirrup may be called for; in contrast, on a more slightly built, narrow horse, you may prefer a shorter stirrup. Proper stirrup adjustment, then, is really a matter of function and feel. If you ride daily and do not have a trainer or ground man to help you, check stirrup length against the ankle bone several times a week.

There are two further points on stirrup adjustment which, though obvious, are often overlooked.

Frequent mounting stretches the leather on the left side, especially if the leathers are new or made of rawhide. To compensate for this, a meticulous horseman changes leathers often from one side of the saddle to the other.

The other point has to do with adding holes to the stirrup leathers. Holes should be punched at carefully measured intervals, otherwise

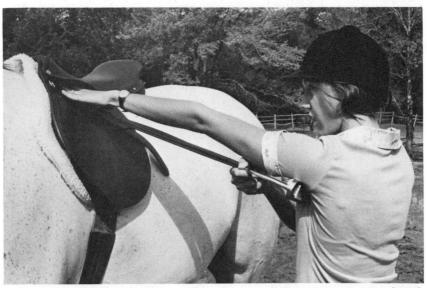

ABOVE: *Adjusting length of stirrup from the ground.* LEFT: *Correct stirrup length for jumping.* RIGHT: *Correct stirrup length for work on the flat.*

Girth adjustment. LEFT: *Incorrect.* RIGHT: *Correct.*

correct and even adjustment of the stirrups is impossible. To add holes to your stirrup leathers, remove them from the saddle and, using a ruler, mark the half-inch or one-inch points where you want the holes to be.

It is important for the rider to know how to adjust the stirrups and girth while mounted without losing control of the horse. It should be done smoothly, especially on a nervous horse who might startle at the movement of the saddle skirt as it is pulled up, or at the rider's slight shift in weight as he adjusts the stirrup.

Stirrup leathers adjustment. LEFT: *Incorrect. An accident about to happen.* RIGHT: *Correct.*

To make either adjustment, first take both reins in the hand opposite to the side where the adjustment will be made. To adjust the girth, keep your foot in the stirrup and pull the skirt of the saddle up, holding it there with your knee. Reach down, loosen the girth buckle and move it to the desired position; use your index finger to press the tongue of the buckle into the correct hole in the leather.

Likewise, to adjust the stirrup, put the foot home in the stirrup iron and draw the leg up a little bit with the knee away from the saddle. Reset the buckle with your free hand, using your index finger to move the tongue into the proper hole.

4

Riding Position and Aids

After you have mounted and settled yourself gently into the saddle, position yourself correctly for riding. To be sure that you are not sitting too far back in the saddle, allow a good hand's width between your seat and the edge of the saddle (assuming the saddle is of proper fit). Now, rest your thigh, knee, and upper calf on the horse, and press your heels down, back, and in toward the horse's body. The stirrup iron should be under the ball of your foot.

A rider's upper body depends entirely on his seat and legs for support. You should sit lightly on the horse, stretching your back up as you stretch your heels down. Always look ahead, in the direction you are going, not down at your hands or at the horse. When you hold your elbow in front of your hip, the reins will be the right length and your hands should be just above the horse's withers. Hold

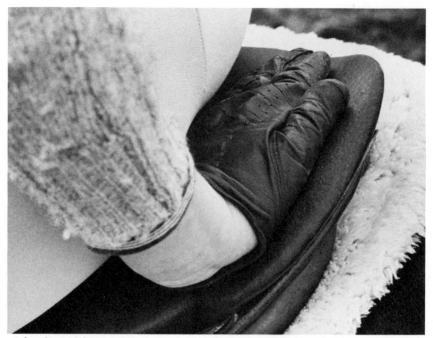

A hand's width of saddle behind the seat assures that the rider is not sitting too far back on the saddle.

your hands so that the flat of the hand is halfway between vertical and horizontal, at about a 45-degree angle. (Flat hands and upright hands tend to be rigid hands.) There should be no bending of the wrists in or out; leave them straight and relaxed. Some people prefer to control the single rein with the little finger, but I think a rider has a more secure feel if he gathers the rein between the third and fourth (little) finger, while passing it out of his hand and holding it snug between the thumb and index finger. With a pelham or double bridle, the little finger separates the two reins.

While a correct position should be maintained at all times, this is not the same as keeping a rigid, mechanical seat. We have all seen examples of the posed, pretty rider who is concentrating so hard on appearance that he is oblivious to what the horse is doing. This is not what is meant by correct position.

At all times, you should accommodate your seat—your center of gravity—to the horse's center of gravity and to the specific kind of riding being done. The upper body is more upright at slower, more collected gaits. But when galloping cross-country or when showing

ABOVE AND LEFT: *Proper basic position at the halt. Head, shoulder, hip, and heel are in line. Another line runs from the elbow to the horse's mouth. About two-thirds of the rider's weight is in her heels and one-third in her seat.* BELOW: *Correct position of the upper body.*

your hunter around an outside course, you take a more forward position. George Morris describes these two positions as "three-point contact" (the seat and the legs) and "two-point contact" (the legs only). In his classes he teaches riders to distinguish between these two balanced seats by showing them how to post "behind the motion"—essentially, up and down—and how to post "with the motion"—essentially, forward and back. A goal of the low intermediate

LEFT: *Sitting too far back in the saddle. The rider is way behind the center of gravity and her feet are too far out in front of her.* OPPOSITE, LEFT: *Back and shoulders too rounded. She is leading with her chin. She needs to stretch up and feel her shirt collar with the back of her neck to straighten her upper body.* OPPOSITE, RIGHT: *Back too stiffly arched. She needs to stretch her back up and imagine she has a pin in her belt buckle.*

rider is to be equally comfortable in both these positions and in all positions between them, since all riding situations require the use of one position or the other. (For a complete and fine explanation of upper-body angulation, refer to Mr. Morris's book, *Hunter Seat Equitation*.)

Here are some exercises to help you develop a good basic position.

○ For a deep heel and proper leg position: Rise slightly in the

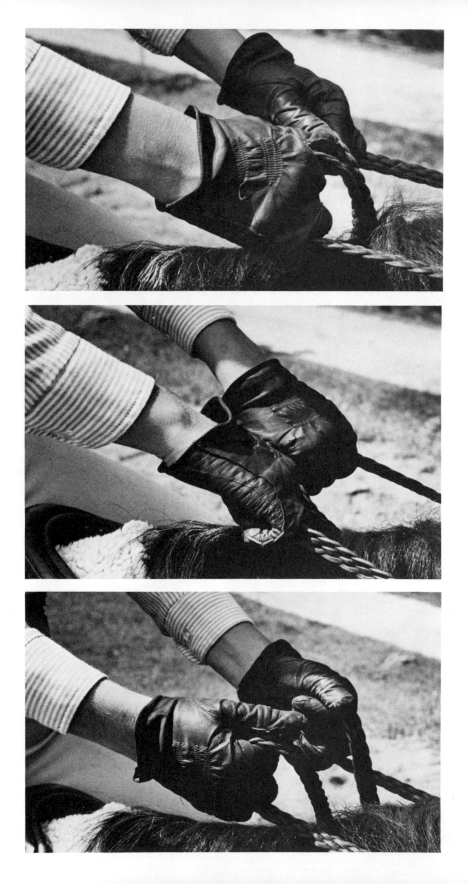

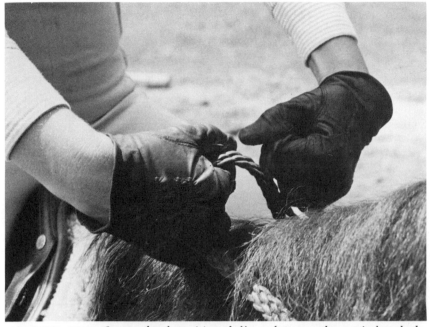

OPPOSITE, TOP: *Correct hand position, halfway between the vertical and the horizontal.* CENTER: *Flat hands are stiff hands.* BOTTOM: *Upright hands also tend to be rigid hands.* ABOVE: *Wrists cocked out.* BELOW: *Wrists cocked in.*

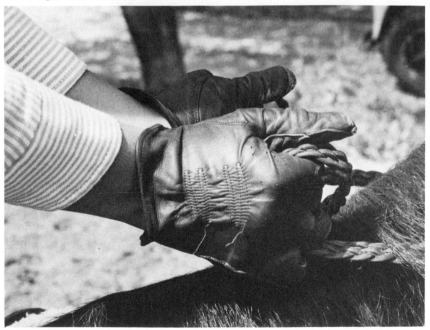

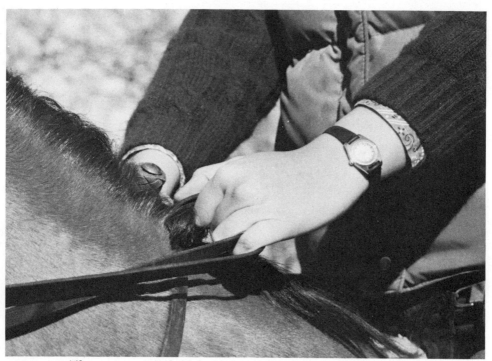

The proper way to hold double reins. The snaffle rein goes around the little finger; the curb, between the ring finger and the little finger.

saddle and press the heels firmly down and back. This exercise cannot be repeated too often by beginners, intermediates, and even advanced riders.

○ To develop and strengthen the lower leg: Assume the half seat, or two-point contact, jumping position, resting the hands one-third of the way up the horse's neck.

○ To develop a deep seat, secure three-point contact, a supple back, and strong lower leg: Ride without stirrups. (When riding without stirrups, pull the buckle down from the stirrup bar 5 or 6 inches before crossing the stirrups in front of the saddle. This prevents the lump of the buckle from interfering with the correct position of the leg.) Hold the leg in the same position as if you were riding with the stirrups. A common tendency is for the knees to come up in front of the body, pushing the rider's seat back toward the cantle of the saddle. Check this often by holding the front of the saddle and drawing your seat toward the pommel. Concentrate on pressing your knees

Slightly perched in the saddle, on the verge of being ahead of the center of gravity. Almost all her weight is in her heels and virtually none in the saddle. Perhaps she is just rising slightly at this moment to press her weight into her heels.

ABOVE: *Posting behind the motion.* BELOW: *Posting with the motion. Both angles are correct and riders should be comfortable with both.*

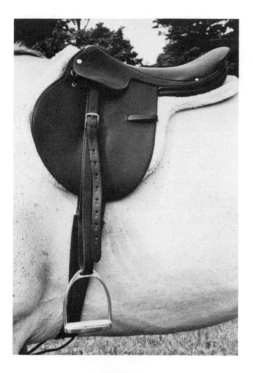

ABOVE, LEFT: *Stirrup leathers pulled down before crossing.* ABOVE, RIGHT: *Stirrups properly crossed in front of saddle for work without stirrups.* LEFT: *Proper position without stirrups. Her reins may be a little long.*

down as you draw your toes up. Take care not to balance yourself by pulling on the horse's mouth.

○ For suppling the lower leg: Drop the stirrups and rotate the
foot slowly. This prevents the ankle joint from becoming stiff
and rigid.

○ For suppling the upper body: (1) Bend over and touch the
mane of the horse with your forehead. (2) Lie back with
your head on the horse's rump then sit up, being careful not
to lose leg position as you do so. (3) Take the reins securely
in one hand and place the other hand on your head or hip, then
rotate the arm slowly from front to back.

Obviously some of these exercises could startle the horse if done
strenuously or abruptly. Proceed slowly and quietly, soothing the
horse as you go along.

Any of these exercises can be done while you are working alone
or in a group lesson. An even more effective way to achieve a good,
balanced seat is working on the longe line without reins or stirrups.
Exercise in this way when there is someone available to work with.

The Rider's Aids

LEGS.   In most situations, you will use one of two leg positions.
The first position, just behind the girth, is used for pressing the
horse forward and for bending him in the turns. The second position,
about a hand's width behind the girth, is used to displace the horse's
hindquarters (as in the turn on the forehand), or to correct improper
displacement of the hindquarters (as when a horse loses his hindquarters to the outside on a turn).

HANDS.   Essentially, good hands are sympathetic hands, but not
permissive hands. In other words, a good rider makes judicious use
of the various rein aids (discussed below), either responding with
softness when the horse obeys, or insisting on obedience when the
horse evades the aids.

EYES.   Good eye control is so essential to good riding that I have
come to think of the rider's eyes as very significant aids. For example,
watch a rider in the show-jumping ring. Coming around a turn
toward a jump, he or she is looking *at the jump* and thus can choose
a line and then judge the distance. This rider also sees with peripheral vision the boundaries of the ring and the points where he plans
to turn.

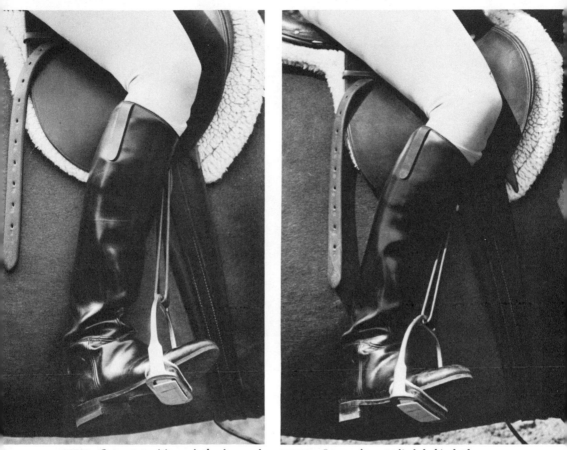

LEFT: *Correct position of the lower leg.* RIGHT: *Lower leg applied behind the girth.*

Body control of both the rider and the horse is governed to a large extent by the use of the rider's eyes. An example of improper use of the eyes is the rider who looks down over the top of a fence in taking a jump; this causes the rider to duck—to drop his or her weight on one side of the horse or the other, which in turn throws the horse off balance. Many problems of upper-body angulation can be corrected by doing eye-control exercises of the sort described in chapter 6.

VOICE.　The voice is a supplementary aid, but nonetheless an important one. Every horse should be taught to respond to the cluck and the "whoa." You can use the cluck to move him forward,

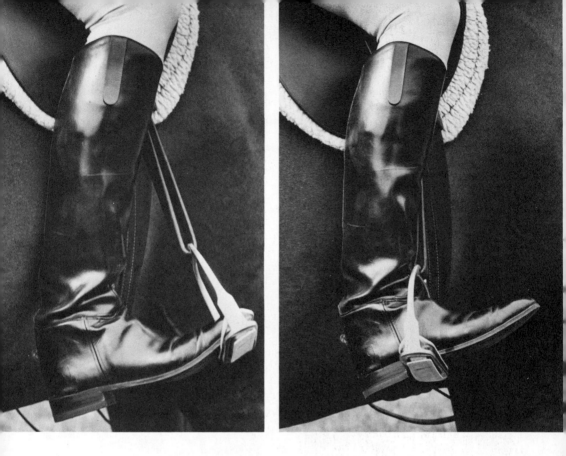

when closing the leg would make him quick or tense. The "whoa" settles him, when taking hold of his mouth might make him tense or worried. A sensitive horse responds well also to the tone of the rider's voice, and this can be especially effective in combination with the other aids—legs and/or hands.

Sometimes you merely need to get the horse's attention. It doesn't really matter what you say—"C'mon" or "Pay attention" or whatever—this use of the voice can be enough to capture a green horse's interest when he is looking outside the ring at a balloon or a goat or some other intriguing object.

The growl is another effective voice aid that works especially well on the paper tigers of the equine species. Many would-be bullies cower when you growl at them. It even works pretty well on the real bullies who buck if you get after them with a stick. If a horse tries to intimidate you by bouncing around a lot after he has done something bad, try growling at him. Sound very fierce and he may back off.

In clinics I've found that the conscious use of the voice can have

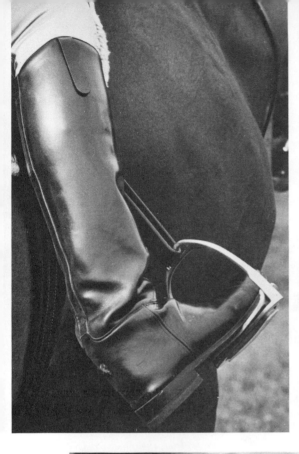

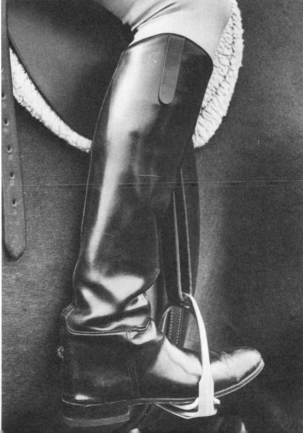

OPPOSITE, LEFT: *Too much on the toe. The rider risks losing her stirrup iron altogether. This precarious position is seen too often in the show ring today.* OPPOSITE, RIGHT: *Foot too far through the stirrup, or "home." A secure position for fox hunters and cross-country riders, but no softness or elasticity is possible.* ABOVE, LEFT: *On the knee and toe wtih no calf contact. This is an insecure as well as an ineffective lower-leg position.* ABOVE, RIGHT: *The ankle bent out away from the horse. Also a weak position.* LEFT: *Not enough weight in the rider's heel. A weak lower-leg position.*

ABOVE, LEFT: *Use of the direct rein for stopping.* ABOVE, RIGHT: *Use of the indirect rein for a left bending.* LEFT: *Use of the neck rein to turn the horse sharply to the right.* BELOW, LEFT: *Use of the leading rein to lead the horse toward the left.* BELOW, RIGHT: *Use of the pulley rein for an emergency stop.*

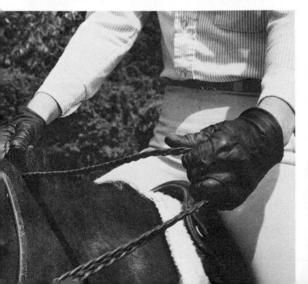

beneficial side effects. Using this aid can change his attitude toward himself and his horse. The timid rider who develops a mean-sounding growl usually becomes on the whole a more aggressive and demanding rider. In contrast, an aggressive rider who uses words to soothe an uptight horse often becomes a more soft and sympathetic rider.

Rein Aids

The rider should know and be able to apply any of the five common rein aids.

The first is the *direct rein*. Here the reins work directly from front to rear and are used for stopping and turning the horse.

The second rein aid is the *indirect rein*, which is used to displace the horse's weight from one side to the other. The indirect rein in front of the horse's withers goes from the inside corner of the horse's mouth, along his neck, toward the rider's outside hip; the horse is moving on one track, but his weight is displaced to the outside. The indirect rein behind the horse's withers displaces his weight from the inside shoulder to the outside haunch, so that he is then moving on two tracks—forward and toward the outside. In using the indirect rein, you should not raise your hands or cross your hands over the horse's withers. If you feel your hands crossing the horse's withers, then your reins are probably too long.

The indirect rein can be used on turns by shifting both hands slightly toward the outside; this prevents a horse from falling in on his inside shoulder or, worse yet, cutting in on a turn. (Bernie Traurig, one of America's most talented and knowledgeable riders of hunters and jumpers, has used the indirect rein extensively on his horses with the result that they are beautifully balanced laterally as well as longitudinally.)

A third rein aid often used is the *bearing rein;* cowboys call it the *neck rein*. This rein is applied abruptly against the horse's neck to encourage him to turn sharply. It is often used by riders of jumpers in time classes, where quick turns are essential. Milder use of the bearing rein is essential with a horse that tends to bulge toward the outside (usually toward the barn, or home) on his turns.

Another rein aid more practical than classical and seldom used in the hunter or equitation ring, is the *leading* or *opening rein*. A jumper rider may use this aid over the top of a fence to lead the horse toward the next turn but without interfering with the horse's use of his head and neck over the jump. In schooling, this rein is useful to counteract a horse's tendency to drift to one corner of the jump. Also, it works well on colts, softly guiding them to go straight as they go forward.

The fifth important rein aid is the *pulley rein,* which is used to stop a horse that is out of control. This is strictly an emergency measure. Practice it at home in case you ever need it. With shortened reins, press one hand down hard on the horse's neck while pulling up and back with the other hand.

Under normal circumstances, one would never have to use a pulley rein on an obedient, well-schooled horse. However, it is a horse's instinct to run away when startled, and in such an instance you may have cause to resort to this severe stopping device.

Punishment and Reward

Punishment, in the very broad sense of the word, is the rider's use of any active aid in order to exert his will over the will of the horse. Reward is the absence of punishment. Here is a simple example of the use of punishment and reward. If a horse wants to go

A quick pat for a job well done. This horse has a wonderful temperament, steady, generous, and reliable. He is just as nice as he looks.

Lydia Theurkauf on Royal Patrick and Best Mistake. Lydia had a wonderful natural instinct for following her horses in the air long before riders and trainers became so concerned about correct upper body angulation. ABOVE: *Patrick, her equitation horse, is a rather flat jumper; he prefers his rider to sit up a little, to have a slightly open angle.* BELOW: *On the other hand, Mistake, her hunter, leaves the ground with a tremendous thrust and rounds his back in classic form. Hence Lydia has closed her angle somewhat in order to follow the arc of his jump.*

Bob Foster

faster than his rider chooses, the rider pulls on the reins, causing the bit to press against the horse's mouth—on the corners of the mouth if it is a snaffle bit, on the bars if it is a pelham or double bridle. When the horse goes slower in response to the punishment, the rider rewards him by softening or relaxing his hand.

Learning the correct degree of punishment to apply is a large part of one's education as a horseman, for each horse and each situation must be dealt with differently. For instance, a young horse that spooks and stops at a strange jump should be given what is called the second to third degree of punishment: a light swat with the stick and he is made to face the jump. A more experienced horse that spooks suddenly and stops receives the fourth to sixth degree of punishment: he gets a couple of good cracks and is made to face the jump. A confirmed pig of a stopper gets the eighth to tenth degree of punishment: he must face the jump and take between five and ten really hard cracks with the whip.

As a rule, resistances come in pairs, so while you are correcting one disobedience, be prepared for the next. This second disobedience usually is committed in anticipation of the punishment for the first. For example, if a horse stops at a jump and is punished with the whip, he will next want to run away from the whip. You must be ready to pull him up before he gets away from you.

The growl, a very stern "Grrr," is an effective method of disciplining roguey horses or bullies. Horses that react by bouncing around when punished with the stick are often quite astonished by the growl.

Reward can accomplish as much as punishment. The best riders know this; they have a wonderful knack for getting their horses to like them and to try extra hard for them. The team of Sandsablaze and Buddy Brown comes to mind. This little horse has tried his heart out for Buddy and frequently won against world-class jumpers.

By reward I do not mean treating a horse as a pet, or feeding it lots of sugar and carrots. The rapport is intangible. Perhaps the best way to define it is to give you an illustration of the opposite quality, the case of a rider I once had who showed no sympathy whatsoever with her horses. Though she had talent as a rider, she was demanding to a fault. Her horses needed strong bits to stop them and spurs to make them go. She never rewarded her horses with so much as a pat on the neck. I had the feeling that they didn't like her. And probably I was right.

Buddy Brown and Sandsablaze. Buddy and "Pappy" have a truly unique rapport.
When Sandsablaze was Buddy's equitation horse several years ago, he seemed to
struggle to jump 3 feet 6 inches; now he regularly wins Grand Prix. Good rides
day in and day out have made Sandsablaze an extraordinarily capable jumper,
capable of winning in world class company.

Never lose your temper, no matter how frustrating and disobedient a horse may be. Emotion itself is not undesirable in a
rider. In fact, I find that young people who learn to control their
emotions eventually make the best riders. Instead of wasting their
emotions on temper tantrums directed toward the horse, they learn
how to push themselves toward achieving the results they want.

What is unacceptable is a loss of temper that takes itself out on
the horse. An angry rider usually yanks his horse around, punishing
the horse in the mouth. Such action only makes the horse worried
about the mouth as well as tense and upset in general. Months,
years, even a lifetime of good work with a horse can be undone by a
single outburst of temper. Rather than tolerate such behavior, I've
told many a young rider to put his horse away for the day.

5

Work on the Flat

Both horse and rider can benefit from work on the longe (pronounced *lunge*) line. This is a form of exercise used to develop balance and control. Longeing is also done to work down a horse that is too fresh for one reason or another. (Sometimes lack of exercise for several days, or even a sudden change in the weather can cause a quiet horse to become rather unmanageable.) Hence, any serious rider should know how to longe his or her horse properly. Keep in mind, however, that while work on the longe line is of great value, it should always be considered an introduction to, not a substitute for, proper work on the flat.

The proper equipment for longeing includes the following: longe line, longeing whip, and side reins. When longeing in side reins, use a plain snaffle bit; other bits are too sharp and will cause the horse to drop behind the bridle. Run the longe line through the inside ring of the bit from outside to inside and then over the top of the horse's head and snap it to the outside ring of the bit. Next, the side reins, fairly loose at first, should be attached to the bit and the girth, with the inside rein one or two holes shorter than the outside rein. If you longe with the saddle on, remove the stirrup irons or else tie them up securely so they don't flap against the horse's sides.

The Horse

Teaching a horse to longe is best done with two people. One leads the horse around until he understands that he is expected to circle the person who holds the longe line and whip. Be very careful when starting any horse off on the longe line. A fresh horse or a young colt may dart away, kicking up his heels in his exuberance and putting the person on the other end of the line in considerable danger. And a rider should never be longed on a horse that is not thoroughly familiar with the procedure.

The person longeing the horse should hold the line in the front hand (the left hand if the horse is going to the left) with the whip in the other hand (see illustrations). The longe line corresponds to the rider's hands; the whip, to his legs. In moving around, the horse should learn to keep an even distance from the person longeing him; in other words, the circle should be round, not lopsided. To prevent the horse from cutting in, hold the longe whip at his shoulder rather than in the normal position, behind him. The horse should learn to walk, trot, and canter equally well in both directions. Teach the horse to respond briskly to the two essential voice commands, the cluck and the "whoa." Don't belabor the point with voice commands to "walk," "trot," and "canter." Though some horses pick up such commands quickly, the tone of your voice is more important than what you say.

Cavalletti

Longeing a horse over a rail on the ground or over a series of rails approximately 3 feet apart, called cavalletti, helps develop co-ordination by loosening and strengthening the horse's muscles. Most work over the cavalletti is done at the walk and trot. Cantering over

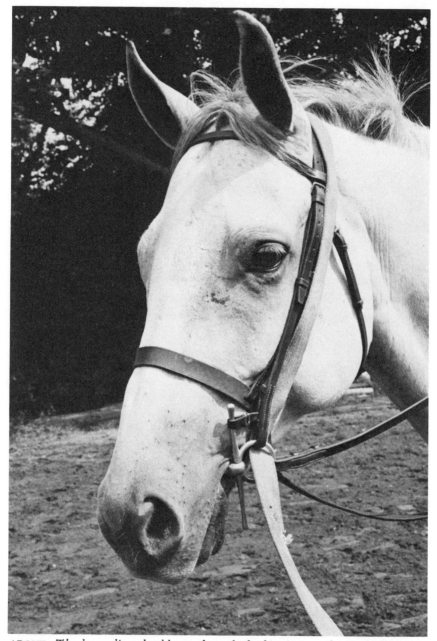

ABOVE: *The longe line should run through the bit ring on the inside then over the horse's poll and snap to outside ring.* OPPOSITE, TOP: *Reins snapped to saddle D for work on longe line without reins.* OPPOSITE, CENTER: *Side reins snapped to girth buckle for work on longe line.* OPPOSITE, BOTTOM: *Stirrups properly tied up for longeing a horse without the rider.*

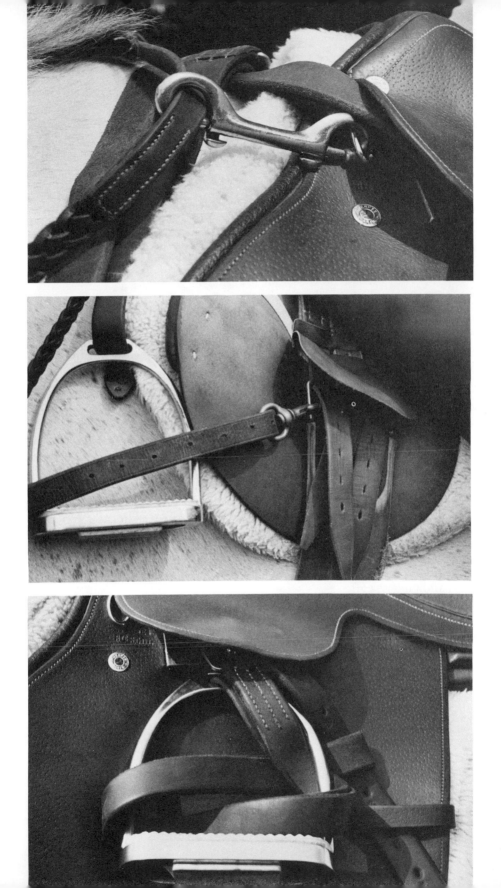

Longeing a green horse in the bitting rig to help him balance himself better. The side reins are fastened low, as the horse, new to us, was very stiff and high-handed. Normally they are attached to a higher ring.

a single rail is a good exercise to teach the horse to adjust his center of gravity. In general, horses that work over rails on the ground seem to develop a certain surefootedness and a better control over their balance. Work over cavalletti can be done both on the longe line and under saddle.

The Rider

Once the horse is thoroughly accustomed to being longed, then and *only then* can a rider ride him on the longe line. After mounting, the rider should grasp the back of the saddle with his inside hand (*inside* denotes the side toward the center of the circle, that is, the left side if the horse is going to the left) and the pommel with the outside hand. You should hold yourself toward the pommel with the outside hand (see illustration), continuing to do so until you feel that your body has gained some independence of your hands.

Then you can do all the exercises mentioned in the previous chapters: hands on head, hands on hips, rotating arms, touching head to knee and hands to toes; you can also rotate your entire body toward the center of the circle and away, with your arms outstretched. You should check your position often to make sure that you are not sliding back toward the cantle or drawing your knees up in front of you.

As you gain confidence, you can be longed over low jumps. At first you should hold on securely to the horse's mane. Soon your legs will be strong enough to allow you to maintain your position and follow the horse in the air as he jumps without holding on. My advanced riders like to try closing their eyes and feeling the horse gather himself for the jump. Most of them can follow the horse's thrust pretty well. The side reins always should be removed before jumping; otherwise they will discourage the horse from using his head and neck.

Hold pommel and cantle for security.

ABOVE: *Doing turning in and out exercises. The horse is rather behind bridle and his hindquarters are not sufficiently engaged.*

OPPOSITE, ABOVE: *Jumping with arms outstretched. Here her foot is just a little too far through the stirrup iron. Better that than too much on the toe in which case she risks losing the stirrup altogether. Notice the stirrup leather is twisted (incorrectly). It can happen easily if you've been working without stirrups.*

OPPOSITE, BELOW: *Lying back on horse's rump. Have someone hold the horse's head until he is not alarmed by this exercise. (Some horses simply will never tolerate such foolishness, so use judgment here!)*

Work on the Flat

After you have mounted and walked the horse around for a few minutes, start the day's work with an energetic ordinary trot. This warms you and the horse up and puts you both in a lively, forward moving gear. If you find on the first trot that your horse is very fresh and just not paying attention, I think it is a good idea to dismount and put him on the longe line for five or ten minutes. Your horse should never learn that he can cavort around and even buck you off if he feels like it.

To avoid the possibility of having to deal with a very fresh horse, try turning him out for an hour or two every day before you ride. Horses were never meant to spend their lives cooped up in a box stall, and they are always much more mellow if they get some

Nicely balanced strong trot. The horse in a good frame between hands and legs.

freedom, even in a small paddock, for several hours a day. We have a couple of horses that behave best at the horse show if they spend the night before in the paddock. Unfortunately, one of the biggest problems of showing horses today is that they must travel from show to show with no chance to be turned out.

Longitudinal Work: Pace Control

During that warmup trot, you should concentrate first on regulating the horse's pace at the ordinary trot. Pace control is a primary concern of any rider, regardless of his level of training. The horse should maintain the same pace all the way around the ring, with the rider anticipating and correcting any change of pace. Without

Nicely balanced canter. Again, a good frame.

this regulation by the rider, the horse will probably want to go faster in the direction of home (the barn) and slower away from home. The sensitive rider understands the horse's point of view and counteracts his increases and decreases even before they occur.

If the horse seeks to get above his pace—to go too fast—then hold him lightly with your leg and exert some pressure on his mouth. When the horse responds and decreases to the requested ordinary trot, respond by softening your hand. If a rider neglects to soften his or her hand and keeps hanging on the horse's mouth, the horse soon learns that there is no reward for responding to the hand and leans against it or ignores it altogether. If the horse's good responses are not rewarded, he eventually learns to pay no attention to any directions from the rider.

In contrast, if the horse is sluggish and wants to go more slowly than the lively ordinary trot you seek, then close your legs and press your horse forward into your hand until the desired pace is achieved.

Maintaining an even pace all the way around the ring is not as easy as it sounds, because most horses do not have much natural instinct to go at an even pace. The rider's sense of rhythm is what

The horse a little behind the rider. He is behind the bridle as well as her leg and her body.

Here the horse is resisting by pushing his nose up in the air. The correction is to close the leg.

helps to regulate the horse's pace; some riders find it helpful to count 1–2, 1–2, 1–2 while trotting along.

I think that maintaining an even pace is especially important when riding very green horses. They are often gawky and uncoordinated, so the balance and rhythm of the trot has to be established by the rider. Moreover, an even pace encourages concentration, which is necessary with green horses since their attention wanders if they are not reminded often about the job at hand.

Transitions: Increases and Decreases

Once you have established and can maintain the ordinary trot, practice some transitions within each gait and between gaits. For instance, decrease your horse's pace to the sitting trot, or increase his pace to the strong trot. Also, you must teach him smooth transitions from one gait to another, for instance, from the walk to the canter. (This, of course, does not apply to the green horse, who should learn first to do all his transitions through the sitting trot. From walk to canter and vice versa are too abrupt, so he should be asked to canter out of a sitting trot. Later, as he gains balance and understanding, you can demand more prompt responses.)

Decreasing the paces, a rider often loses the horse—that is, forgets to keep the legs on the horse and takes the horse's mouth with the hand. You won't make this mistake if you remember always to have your horse in a "frame," the frame being defined by your hands and your legs—*both* hands and *both* legs at all times. The frame, however, should always be light and soft, not rigid and mechanical.

Straightness

The ability to ride in a straight line is a very important concern for the serious rider. The horse has little tendency to keep straight unless he is urged to do so by his rider. Practice straightness at all gaits, at the halt, and while backing up. The long sides of the rectangular ring, the center line, and the diagonal lines across the ring are where the horse can be encouraged to go straight. Fix your attention on some focal point and ride directly toward it. Be alert to any deviations your horse makes from the straight line and correct them—if possible, even before he wanders from the line. After years of practice, you will learn to ride a straight line; in the meantime marvel at the precision of world-class dressage riders whose horses move down the center line with not one foot out of place.

Handedness

Like people, horses are either left-handed or right-handed. It seems that most horses are left-handed, and various reasons are cited for this. Some people claim that horses are left-handed because most people who work with them are right-handed. We lead them on the left side, put on their halters and tack from the left, and mount from the left. Consequently, from an early age, much of a horse's attention is directed to the left side. In addition, racing is done counter-clockwise—to the left—and thus horses that have raced are more comfortable going to the left.

For whatever reasons, a horse usually prefers and goes better in one direction than the other. Whether to the left or the right, he will be softer and more responsive on that side. A good principle of training is to work the good direction first and the bad direction longer; spend, say, 10 to 15 percent of your time on the good direction and the balance on the other direction.

As part of the softening process, alternate your directional work with half-turns, figure eights, and serpentines. Sometimes if a horse is soft and relaxed in one direction, this will carry over briefly, and then eventually longer, to the other direction. However, expect him to resist most when going from his good to his bad direction. If you can achieve softness and obedience in this specific situation, it is a milestone indeed.

Lateral Work: Bending

The object of this work is to teach the horse to bend his body from head to tail to conform to the arc of his turns and circles. In the beginning, lead him with the outside rein to prevent him from falling in on the turn, and at the same time apply the indirect inside rein and the inside leg to hold him out as you bend him around the inside leg. The outside leg should rest against his side and prevent his hindquarters from falling outside the arc of the turn or the circle. Once the horse understands and begins to bend properly, the outside leading rein can be replaced with a steady rein along his neck on the outside.

The circle is essentially a continuation of the bending initiated in the turn. When circling, make sure the horse's body bends around your inside leg so that the bend of his body corresponds to the arc of the circle. Hence, his body is bent more when executing smaller circles, and less when making larger circles. Intermediate riders who have just learned to bend their horses tend to overdo the bending.

The two evasions you will have to deal with most often when turning and circling are cutting in and bulging out. Keep your hands close together so that the reins frame his neck. To counteract your horse's tendency to cut in on his turns, apply a strong inside leg and

ABOVE: *The horse correctly bent around the rider's leg to parallel the arc of the circle.* BELOW: *The horse incorrectly bent. The rider has pulled the horse's head to the outside, and he is falling in on his inside shoulder.*

The counter canter around a turn. The horse should be bent to the outside, because he is on the outside (or counter) lead.

inside indirect rein. Also, leaning a bit to the outside often helps. On the other hand, if he bulges out, you must hold him more with your outside leg and the outside rein along his neck—almost a neck rein such as the cowboys use. Expect him to try to cut in on the far turns, the ones farthest from the in gate—the barn, "home"—and to bulge out on those nearest the in gate. The thinking rider anticipates these evasions and corrects them before they occur.

For the sake of accuracy and promptness, it is helpful to train in an enclosed area where the traditional dressage letters are posted as shown in the diagrams. But do not confine your work to the enclosed area. Your horse will become bored. Vary the surroundings and the training; horses are people too. Ride for a change in an open field, using an imaginary rectangle. See if you can be prompt and accurate when there are only invisible points to ride to. If your horse has been drilled a lot in the ring, ride him cross-country once in a while. Practice bending and straightening him as you go through the woods. He'll enjoy the change and so will you.

Schooling Exercises for Daily Flatwork

○ Ordinary trot to warm up. Don't be too demanding the first few minutes.

○ Transitions through the trot (sitting, ordinary, strong trot) on circles and straight lines. Be sure the horse is straight on the lines and the arc of his body parallels the arc of the circles and turns.

○ Cantering. A beginner often uses lateral aids, outside rein and outside leg to press his horse into a canter. These very primitive aids also work well with the very green horse. Later, such lateral aids are replaced by diagonal aids, the inside indirect rein to bend the horse slightly in the direction he is going accompanied by outside leg behind the girth. (A gentle nudge with the outside leg before you actually ask for the canter will engage your horse's hocks as well as get his attention.) Practice transitions between the ordinary and strong canter as well.

○ Transitions from one gait to another, including the halt and the back. Be sure to use both reins and both legs for all transitions, upward and downward.

○ Halts. Still, immobile, straight, close your *leg* and your hand to halt your horse. Stretch your back up as you close the leg and the hand.

○ Half-halts. The half-halt is exactly that. The rider asks the horse to halt and, just as he is about to halt, rides him forward. The half-halt, though barely visible, is a simultaneous, coordinated action of the legs, seat, and hands to get the horse's attention and to balance him before executing various movements or transitions to slower or faster paces. The half-halt engages the horse's hindquarters and hence lightens his forehand and his balance in general. Repeated half-halts are very effective when the horse is too sluggish or when he goes too fast. It is a quick, short gathering of the horse, an assertive signal from the rider to the horse to pay attention, to listen to you.

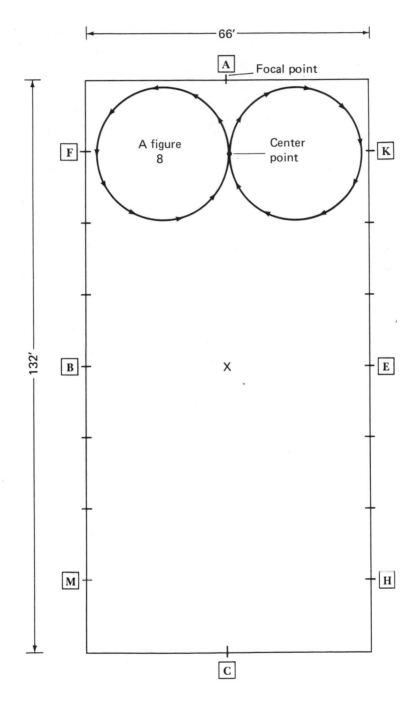

66'

A | Focal point

A figure
8

Center
point

F

K

132'

B | X | E

M | H

C

A figure eight.

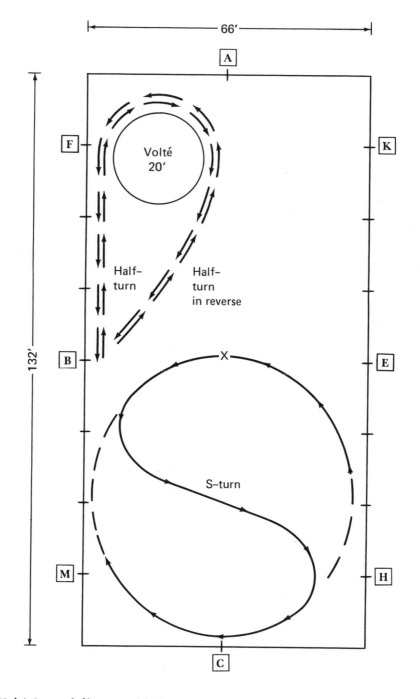

Volté, S-turn, half-turn, and half-turn in reverse.

○ Rein backs. Less experienced riders tend to back their horses by using their hands. More advanced riders close their legs as they close their hands to achieve a more balanced rein back. As the horse yields and backs a step or two, soften the hand. Don't continually choke him. Ask for a few steps at a time at first and be sure to keep him straight. Don't back him every time you halt or he will learn this as his lesson.

○ Circles at all gaits, an exercise in precision. Be sure circles are round, not lopsided. The smallest such exercise, a *volté,* is a circle 20 feet in diameter; it is too small a circle for very green horses. Circles are also good for settling a fresh horse. The S turn through the circle, as from X to C is one way to change direction—bending then straightening one or two strides, and then bending in the other direction. Opening and closing the circle at the trot and canter, using the same mid-point to teach the horse to stay in the "frame" between hands and legs. This exercise makes the rider deal with such lateral evasions as cutting in or bulging out.

○ Changes of direction across the diagonal, as for example in your ring, A–K–X–M–C–H, down the center line, F–A–X–C–H, or across the short side of the ring, K–E–X–B–M. Again, be sure the horse is straight on lines and bent around the turns.

○ Half-turns and half-turns in reverse, at all gaits. For example, to do a half-turn proceed along B just past F right toward A (but never over center line AXC) and back to and past E. For half-turns in reverse, proceed from B toward A (but again not over center line AXC) and then left toward F and finally again past E.

○ Neat, prompt departs into canter from walk and halt with the horse's head bent slightly to the inside as you apply the outside leg.

○ Free, ordinary, unhurried walk. Allow the horse to stretch his head and neck. Use good judgment about giving him a break when working intensively on the flat. Ride and then relax. Ten minutes of concentrated riding is better than thirty minutes of purposeless exercise. Do not work your horse all the time; give him a break every ten to fifteen minutes.

○ Turns on the forehand and haunches. Not hurried, but one step at a time. Eyes up and heels down. Novice riders should

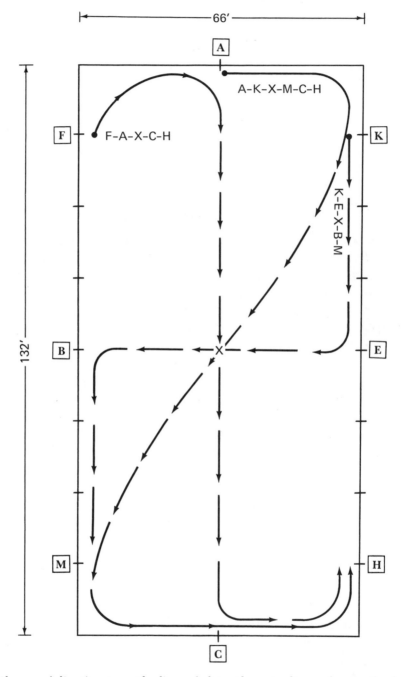

Changes of direction across the diagonal, down the center line, and across the short side.

learn to perform the turn on the forehand. Hold your horse's head gently with the reins. Your inside leg should be on the girth, the outside leg pressing behind the girth to push his hindquarters around his stationary forehand. More advanced riders should know how to execute the turn on the haunches, but they should attempt this exercise first under the guidance of their trainer. The object is for the forehand to describe the arc as the haunches remain stationary. The rider leads the horse with his inside rein and presses his outside rein against the neck as his outside leg on the girth actively presses the horse to make the turn.

O Broken lines and serpentines at all gaits. A broken line can be ridden, for example, from C and H toward X then to K and A. This is a good exercise for practicing eye control: At H look toward X, as you reach X, consciously shift your eyes to K. Serpentine loops must match in length and width—another exercise in precision. Starting at C proceed right past M across the ring to an imaginary point between E and H; at E turn left across X and right again at B; halfway between B and F turn right toward another imaginary point between E and K; proceed past K to A. The horse should be straight on the lines and bent on the turns. Change diagonals and leads upon crossing center line AXC. Do simple changes of lead at the center; more advanced riders can do flying changes or hold one lead throughout the exercise.

O Figure eights at the trot and canter. Practice nice round circles, holding the horse out on circle and looking in to the center point for accuracy. (The "focal point" is on the rail; the "center point," where the change is made, is about 18 feet in from the rail, a little over the radius of the intended circle.) For example, in the ring use as your center point an imaginary point about 18 feet in from A. Facing A, your focal point on the rail, ride two perfectly round circles, one to the right, one to the left. At the canter, do simple or flying changes. If the horse anticipates change, halt four seconds between changes. More advanced riders can perform this exercise on the counter lead.

O Leg-yielding. Leg-yielding is a basic exercise to teach the horse to be obedient to the lateral aids. It supplies him and prepares him for more advanced lateral movements such as the shoulder-in. Leg-yielding basically means bending the horse around the active leg. It can be done on a straight line, on a turn, on a circle, or across the diagonal. Young horses can learn to yield to the leg in early stages of their training. At the turns, the rider can apply the indirect rein with an active inside leg, pressing the horse away from the inside of the ring. Be sure to keep the horse moving forward and be careful not to let his haunches swing too much to the outside, an evasion popular with most horses I know.

○ Shoulder-in. This is one of the most valuable lateral suppling exercises. It can be performed either on a straight line or on a circle, either at the walk or at the sitting trot. More advanced riders can also practice this exercise at the canter. For the left shoulder-in the indirect rein is used along with an active left leg. The horse moves with the left hind leg tracking the right fore. You need help from your trainer to learn to perform this exercise. Intermediate riders should not attempt it on their own, for they risk confusing the horse.

○ Counter canter. Once horse and rider have mastered the canter, it is time to introduce the counter canter, the canter on the outside lead. The best way to introduce the counter canter is upon completion of the half-turn. Instead of changing your lead as you come back to the rail at say E or B, hold the counter lead as you proceed around the ring. To achieve a smooth transition from the walk to the counter canter use a few steps of shoulder-in so that the horse is already bent in the proper direction and balanced properly. In short, ride the counter canter as you would ride the canter; maintain the *same* bend and the *same* seat and use the *same* aids. The counter canter is an excellent suppling and balancing exercise. At first the horse may break or swap off his lead, but take the time to balance him properly and try again. Eventually he will understand what you want. Make big wide turns at first.

○ Flying changes. Be sure the horse's body is completely straight before asking for a change. To teach him flying changes, shift hands to the outside of the turn to displace his weight from his inside shoulder to his outside haunch, meanwhile holding his hindquarters in with the outside leg as well. Then ask for the change with a strong outside leg. Do not let him increase his pace as you ask for the change. Use the rail or the wall of

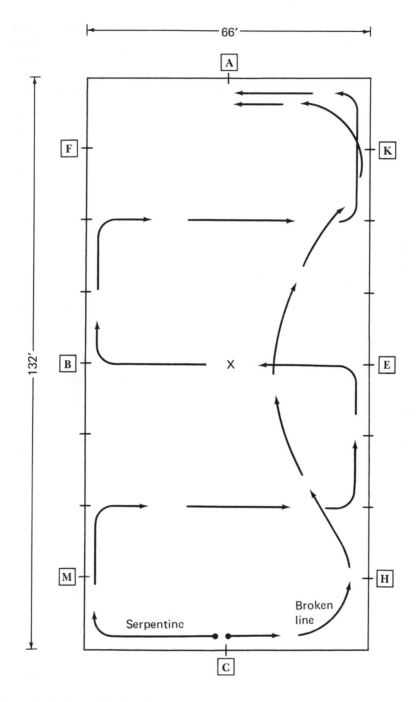

Serpentine loops and broken lines.

the ring to force the change and to prevent the horse from getting away from you. Nowadays, perfect flying changes on course are absolutely essential, even at the intermediate level, so take the time to teach your horse and keep after him until he does them perfectly whenever asked. He may very well get upset until he understands what you want and has the co-

Bernie Traurig, riding Hunting Valley Farm's Singapore. Bernie is among the top riders in the world partly because he spends the time training his horses so they are always perfectly balanced even going down this steep bank. Singapore is a particularly interesting horse to me. He demonstrates how important consistent and conscientious training is to the development of a top jumper.

SUE MAYNARD

ordination to do it. Meanwhile don't be deterred by his getting in a flap. Stay calm and persist until he learns it. The flying change should be attempted first under your trainer's supervision.

○ Simple or flying changes on a line. Be precise about the number of strides between changes. Halt for four seconds between changes if the horse anticipates the change and becomes tense.

○ Complete the day's work with something your horse does well, so that when the work is over he feels good about himself and so do you. Good endings are as important as good beginnings.

○ After finishing the daily work, take the horse for a little relaxing walk, if only around the ring, or down the driveway. End the day on a relaxed note.

Every serious rider should have a definite plan regarding his or her horse's progress and goals. The plan should be fairly well defined but not inflexible. It should combine short-range goals ("This week I want to work on getting more prompt canter departs") with more general long-range goals ("Next year I hope to be able to show him in some jumper classes as well as the equitation").

Your daily program should be directed toward these goals. Essentially the object is to teach the horse to "carry himself," to maintain his balance and rhythm without a lot of obvious direction on the part of the rider. You should remember that practical ridability is your aim. For the hunt seat equitation rider and the trainer of hunters and jumpers, whether this work is called "dressage" or "schooling your horse" or "getting him broke," it is a means and not an end. It is a tool for improving the horse's overall performance.

You should always aim for excellence, but at the same time you should not get bogged down in the pursuit of impossible perfection. If you do, you may never get beyond the sitting trot. Here again, an objective ground man or trainer can provide very helpful guidance.

How Much Work and How Often?

Usually about forty-five minutes is long enough to work most horses. If you find you have to ride much longer than that to accomplish what you want, then perhaps you are demanding too much too soon. Sometimes twenty or thirty minutes is enough. It is a matter of judgment.

How often to ride your horse is also a question of judgment. Most young horses do well being worked four or five days a week; older horses need work two or three days. Jumpers need to be much more fit than hunters, so their training program is more intensive. How often to jump your horse depends, too, on the individual. Green horses need more work over jumps than made horses. Always incorporate flatwork with the jumping, and insist on obedience at all times.

Of course, much of the schooling program depends on the time of the year and your overall plan. Before the start of the show season, your schooling sessions at home will be more concentrated. Horses that are showing every weekend will do better with little or no jumping at home and possibly one or two days a week of working on the flat. Many horses perform at their best at shows if they are simply turned out to relax several hours a day between shows. Remember, your horse is not a machine; drilling him does not necessarily improve his performance. Like any athlete, a horse needs time off to freshen up, especially if he is competing in a heavy schedule of horse shows.

Thoroughbred horses don't need much work to get fit, and over-zealous training can put you on the longeing-fitness merry-go-round. You could find yourself longeing him at the shows in order to work him down, and that the more you work him the fitter he gets and the more you have to longe him to work him down. In schooling at home, you needn't fuss at him if he is a little fresh. Just be sure he is turned out and/or worked down enough for the horse show. Do enough, but not too much.

Bill Steinkraus addresses himself to this question of what to do and how much in his excellent book, *Riding and Jumping.* His comments cannot be improved upon and should be engraved in every aspiring horseman's mind:

> The soundest practice is to make haste, and make the most of our horses, neither slowly nor quickly, but appropriately, at the pace that is appropriate to the particular horse we are riding. It is just as wrong to destroy the freshness and bloom of a gifted horse by repeating endlessly exercises that he has already mastered as it is to demand difficult movements from the horse who cannot do the simple ones correctly. The judgment that enables us to tell one from the other is something that we must work patiently to acquire. It will never be infallible, but it is an essential mark of the horseman, and will always distinguish him from those who merely ride well.

6

Schooling over Jumps

Your jumping program will begin with some very simple exercises. One of the best to do over jumps at home is cantering over a single rail on the ground. Cantering cavalletti helps both rider and horse achieve balance and stability. This can be repeated over and over without pounding the horse. Everything but flight is practiced: approach, takeoff, landing, and departure.

A beginning rider uses the rail to practice his release over the jump. As you approach the rail, feel the horse's mouth; over the rail, release by resting up on the crest of the neck; upon landing, feel the horse's mouth again to prevent him from speeding up. Once you have managed the single rail on a circle, you can work on two rails placed about 60 feet apart. Then the sequence is as follows: feel, release, feel, release, feel.

More advanced riders use the ground rail to practice stride control. Here you practice regulating the horse's pace, balance, and length of stride to meet the rail just right. As you become more versatile you can jump the rail off a short stride or off a long stride. Again, you can use a couple of rails and practice putting a variety of strides between the two rails. For instance, if the rails are 24 feet apart, you can practice putting two or even three strides between the two.

Also over a single rail, you can do exercises to sharpen eye control. Practice looking around the turn to the rail, or practice looking at a point in the center of the ring as you find your distance to the rail with your peripheral vision.

This exercise can be done with a number of rails in various patterns. The rider trots and later canters around the prescribed course, first just rails on the ground and then low jumps, and finally bigger

A nice approach to the cavalletto, or rail on the ground.

Angling a jump, or jumping across it from left to right.

and wider jumps. The serpentine is especially useful for practicing turns; hold the horse out on the turn with the indirect rein and the inside leg, while looking in to judge the distance to the jump.

There are a couple of exercises using just a single fence that are very beneficial. First, trot the fence on a line and stop; then practice jumping the fence back and forth at an angle. Be sure to keep the horse's body straight, especially as the angle becomes sharper. You can halt after each jump, or canter back and forth in a figure eight.

A second exercise over a single fence, but for more advanced riders and made horses, is to jump it off the circle and continue the circle after landing. The leading rein over the top of the jump is helpful in this exercise. The rider then can guide the horse without restricting his jumping mechanism. You must be there with your leg to keep the horse lively; ride forward to the jump and wait at the same

Here the rider is looking to make a right turn and guiding her horse to the right with a leading rein.

time; hands to the outside, holding the horse out and looking in for your distance; you must also be sure at the same time that you do not let the horse bulge out too far. This exercise can be done first at the trot and later at the canter, first over a rail on the ground, then a low vertical, and eventually a low and gradually wider oxer.

Even if you are able to measure distance accurately by walking it on foot, it is best to use a tape measure when setting up gymnastics and related distances at home. Keep the tape measure some place handy to the ring, preferably a dry place, so that you will have it to use when you need it. Experienced riders and trainers often check themselves against the measuring tape. Our olympic team coach, Bert de Nemettry, is never without one.

As a rule of thumb, cavalletti should be spaced 3 to 4 feet apart, depending on the size and stride of the horse; the last of a series of cavalletti in front of a jump should be 9 to 10 feet from the jump. The distance between a no-stride pair of fences should be 10 to 12 feet for trotting, 11 to 13 feet for cantering. For a one-stride gymnastic approached at the trot, 18 feet is about right. In general, multiples of 10 feet work well for gymnastics. A 20-foot distance is comfortable for one stride; 30 feet for two strides; 40 feet for three strides.

The stride of an average size horse is about 12 feet. Hence, most comfortable related distances between the jumps on a course at a horse show are in 12-foot multiples. Course designers with large rings to work in often use 13-foot multiples; this striding works very well if the ring area is large enough. In very small rings, especially indoors, 11½-foot multiples work better, at least for the first line or two. The horse's arc over the fence is usually about 12 feet from the takeoff point to the landing point. In other words, a 60-foot distance between two jumps is usually a comfortable four strides. There is the 6-foot distance from the jump to the landing point, then four 12-foot strides, plus 6 feet from the takeoff point to the base of the jump. Thus, 48 feet is a three-stride distance; 60 feet, four strides; 72 feet, five strides; 84 feet, six strides; 92 feet, seven strides. In-and-outs or combinations consist of two or three jumps with related distances of one or two strides. An average one-stride combination usually runs from 24 feet to 27 feet depending on the situation; two-stride combinations from 32 feet to 38 feet.

For more advanced riders, one of the best exercises in stride control is to set up two jumps, usually a vertical jump and a square oxer, in a straight line with a related distance of, say, 72 feet, a normal five-stride distance. The rider then can practice adding an extra stride, or eventually two strides, keeping his horse very lively as he does so. The point of the exercise is to approach the line with a definite plan. The pace and length of stride should be established before approaching the first fence. If you plan on the normal five strides, you should have a brisk pace but not a long, strung-out stride. After you jump the first fence, you should keep going until you see your distance to the next fence. With some practice, you will see your distance about halfway down the line, between the second and third stride, and can make very minor adjustments then, if necessary, to meet the second fence just right. If you plan to add a stride on such a line with an average-striding horse, you should compress the horse's stride slightly before approaching the first fence, and *as soon as he lands* you should shorten your horse so that he does a steady three strides and then a nice three to the second fence (not a nice three followed by a short three and a pop!). You should then practice the line, varying the strides—six one time, then five, then seven (if you are up to that much compression), and finally five again. The line should be jumped from both directions. It is good to end the exercise with normal forward striding.

Sometimes at home I have my advanced riders do the following exercises to teach them to shorten and lengthen their horses' strides quickly. I set up three fences in a line with, say, 45 feet between the first two and 48 feet between the second and third (or 48 feet between one and two and 50 feet between two and three). Then we work the horses back and forth over these fences. A very good rider on a well-schooled horse should be able to do the difficult exercise of a very long three strides (50 feet) to a very short three (45 feet) and vice versa. (The normal three-stride distance, remember, is 48 feet.)

Schooling Exercises Over Low Jumps (3 feet 3 inches)

Trotting fences discourages anticipation by horse and rider. The rider may hold the half seat as he trots the fence or may post the trot, sitting only the last couple of strides. With horses that need a lot of leg to hold them together, it is better if the rider sits the trot all the way to the jump. I start nearly all sessions with trotting low fences. Departures from the fence are as important as approaches, so upon landing, you should incorporate one of the three following exercises.

○ Stop on a line. Then turn on forehand (novices) or on haunches (more advanced riders). Concentrate on straightness.

○ Shift hands to the outside, press the horse out toward the rail with your inside leg as you bend him around that leg. Halt at the end of the ring.

○ Shift hands to the outside, ask for a flying change if necessary, continue around the turn holding out and looking in toward the next jump. Halt at the jump.

Practice holding the half seat—between jumps as well as over the jumps. An especially effective exercise is to hold the half seat through a series of gymnastics.

ABOVE: *The half seat or jumping position. The rider should rest her hands more solidly on the horse's neck.* BELOW: *Practicing the half seat and the crest release over an imaginary jump.*

Alternate trotting and cantering fences with halts, turns, and lines after the jump to reinforce the horse's obedience.

When schooling, see that the horse remains rideable and obedient between jumps. If he gets above his pace or misses a change of lead, circle him. If he then gets strong after the change, circle again until he settles.

Circling is a wonderful settling device before and after the jump. With a sensitive horse especially, circling works better than pulling him up abruptly when he gets above his pace. Here again, a rider with good judgment will know which horse responds better to circling and which horse needs to be pulled up. A sensitive horse responds better to being circled; a bully needs to be set on his tail—sometimes often.

The schooling program that you follow will, of course, depend mostly on the horse's needs and partly upon the type of practice ring you are able to construct from the equipment and space available. Even with very little space a ring sufficient for a good program can be put up. In the following pages several practice rings are diagrammed and daily programs suggested.

Plan A

Start the day's school with a cross rail: Use any vertical that has an easy and inviting approach. Next do the gymnastic, adding one fence at a time for green horses. Made horses should hop through easily if it is set low—2 feet 6 inches to 3 feet. After you master the gymnastic, jump fence 6 and halt at 7. If you want to practice long approaches jump fences 4 and 3 individually.

If you need to practice turns make up little serpentine exercises: 3 then turn right to 4 and left to 6, or 1 then turn left to 5 and right to 7. Fences 6 to 7 or vice versa provide a good line to practice. The serpentine exercise works well for a fresh or quick horse because the rider can use the turns to settle him.

To practice direct or indirect lines between fences not set on a line use fences 4 and 5. You can go *directly* from one to the next in 3 or 4 strides depending on whether the distance is 48 or 60 feet. You can also go *indirectly* from 4 to 5 or vice versa adding a stride.

The gymnastic can be moved easily to provide a combination; make the distances 24 feet between each of the three jumps. Remember the lines ride shorter toward the ingate than away because the

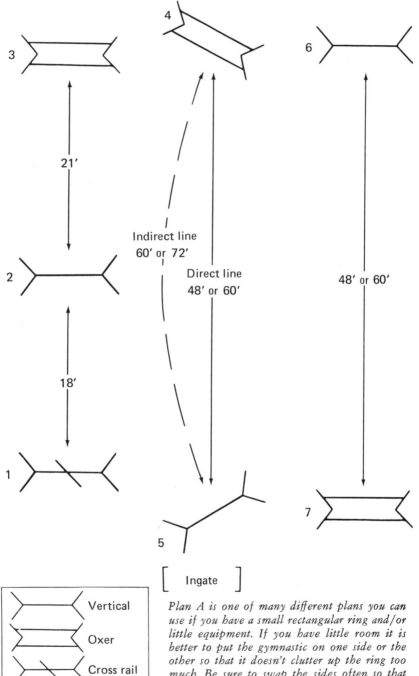

3

4

6

21'

Indirect line
60' or 72'

Direct line
48' or 60'

2

48' or 60'

18'

1

7

5

[Ingate]

Vertical

Oxer

Cross rail

Plan A is one of many different plans you can use if you have a small rectangular ring and/or little equipment. If you have little room it is better to put the gymnastic on one side or the other so that it doesn't clutter up the ring too much. Be sure to swap the sides often so that the horse doesn't always jump from one side.

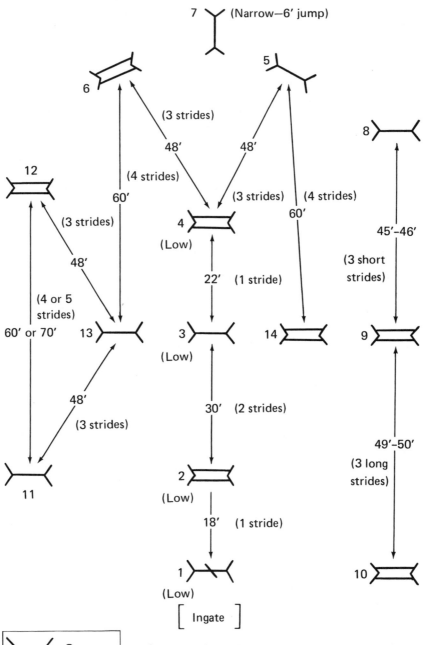

7 Y (Narrow—6' jump)

5

6

8

(3 strides)

48'   48'

(4 strides)

60'   (3 strides) | (4 strides)

12   60'

(3 strides)   4

48'   (Low)

(4 or 5
strides)   22'   (1 stride)   45'–46'

60' or 70'   13   3   14   9   (3 short
strides)

(Low)

48'

(3 strides)

30'   (2 strides)

49'–50'

(3 long
strides)

11   2

(Low)

18'   (1 stride)

1   10

(Low)

[Ingate]

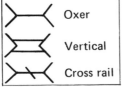

Oxer

Vertical

Cross rail

*Plan B can be used if you have a fairly large square
(or almost square) ring and a lot of equipment. You
can set the jumps so that they can be used in an endless variety of patterns. Set all fences so that they
can be jumped from either direction (with the ex-
ception of the gymnastic 1 through 4).*

horse is more eager going toward "home." Usually oxer-to-vertical lines ride shorter than vertical-to-oxer lines because the oxer carries the horse farther into the line, unless he "hangs up" or is sticky in the air over the oxer.

A number of nice little courses can be made up even with a few jumps. For example, if you do 7–6–5–4–3–2–1 some interesting problems are presented. 7 is an oxer and must be met going forward. The 48- or 60-foot distance to 6 demands a brisk pace but someone with a strong, long striding horse has to make sure he doesn't arrive too early at 6. Conversely someone with a small short striding horse has to hustle along to make sure he gets to 6 in the prescribed number of strides. Next is the long gallop to the vertical where the problem is to keep the horse quiet and soft during the long gallop toward home. The next fence is 4 again with a long gallop but this time away from home and toward an oxer. This is where the timid or sticky horses back off and must be kept going forward. Finally the triple combination 3, 2, and 1 asks whether the horse can shorten to the vertical after going forward to the two oxers. This is a pretty sophisticated combination and less advanced riders and green horses should have fence 3 the vertical and 1 the oxer.

Plan B

A typical day's school would begin with trotting a cross rail (use fence 13 or 11 or 5—any fence will do really). Then jump through the gymnastic. With a green horse, start with the cross rail 1, then one by one build 2, 3, and 4 (having removed those rails before you started jumping). A made horse should hop right through the whole gymnastic set at about 2 feet 6 inches to 3 feet or so. After doing the gymnastic add the vertical fence 5; 3 strides between 4 and 5, then do 1 through 5; go around 7 and jump 6. Next do the gymnastic 1 through 4; 6 and around 7 to 5. Here you are practicing riding a direct line from 4 to 5 or 4 to 6 and you are practicing a nice turn from 5 to 6 or 6 to 5. Obviously you do not want to incorporate all the following patterns in one school but here are some suggestions. To practice single fences jump 13 and/or 14. Both have long approaches and plenty of room afterwards as well. To practice lines, 11 to 12 is 60 or 72 feet so you can work back and forth over those. To practice shortening and lengthening on one line: jump 8, 9 and 10 back and forth. To practice jumping fences on a line that

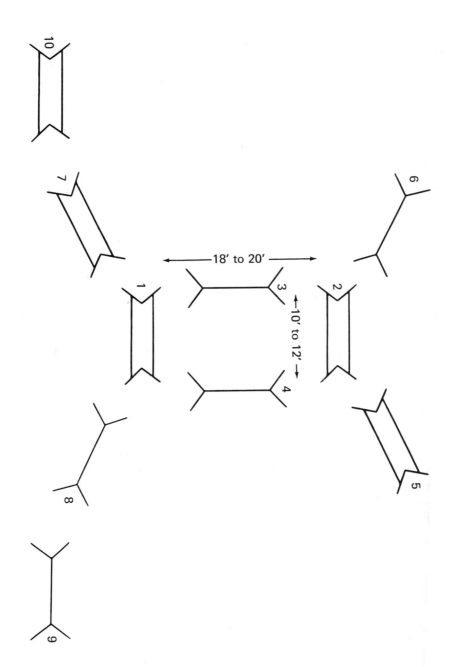

Plan C, the star formation (so named by Captain D'Endrody in his book Give Your Horse a Chance), *is wonderful if you have a very small ring. It is really a compact little grouping of jumps and one I use often when we have little area to work in.*

are not set on a line jump back and forth over 12 to 13, or 13 to 11, or 14 to 5. Circular lines can be incorporated using the end fence 7, going over 12, 7, to 8 and vice versa. S-lines can be put together using fences 8, 15, and 11 or fences 12, 15 and 10. Very sharp turns can be practiced from 13 to 15.

Plan C

Plan C is built around two gymnastics, 1 to 2 and vice versa, where the distance is 18 feet for trotting 1 to 2 (20 feet or more if cantering back and forth). Fences 3 to 4 are verticals, 10 feet apart

Linn Carpenter on Baffles. Linn rode with me for many years as a Junior and now has to fit her riding in with more mundane pursuits like earning a living. She does not have the time to devote to her riding that she did in the past, but she has very good instincts and a strong background in riding basics. She competes in a few shows every year and does just fine. Very good classic form, especially for a part-time rider.

SUE MAYNARD

for trotting, 11 or 12 feet for cantering. Fences 5, 6, 7 and 8 can be jumped individually or as a group depending on the level of horse and rider. For example, indirect lines can be practiced from 5 to 6, 6 to 7, 7 to 8, 8 to 5 and vice versa. A well schooled horse and polished rider could incorporate all four in a circular exercise. Fences 9 and 10 can be added to the original "star" pattern to be jumped individually or incorporated into various lines—6 to 10, or 5 to 9, for instance.

7

Horse and Rider:
Common Difficulties

Riders: Faults over Fences

The most common problems riders have once the horse has left the ground arise from not being able to follow his flight.

The most obvious fault is that the rider is left behind and falls back as the horse takes off. The poor horse then gets a terrible jab in the mouth because the rider is literally hanging on by the reins. There is no quicker way to discourage a horse than to punish his mouth every time he leaves the ground. A rider gets left behind because he does not have enough support from his lower leg. Until he has that support from his leg, he should make it a habit to grab a small piece of mane, one or two strides before the horse takes off.

As his lower leg becomes more secure he can simply rest his hands about halfway up the horse's neck. This is called the "crest release" because the rider releases the horse's head as he rests his hands on the horse's crest. A rider needs a short release over vertical jumps and a long release over oxers. When jumping the latter the horse stretches his neck more and hence needs more freedom of his head.

A rider is "ahead of his horse" when his weight is ahead of the horse's center of gravity. This is also a very serious fault for a number of reasons. The horse is then no longer in a frame between the rider's hands and legs. The immediate result is that the horse falls on his forehand; in other words, he carries much of his weight on his front legs. He then jumps "off his forehand," has difficulty even getting off the ground, and leaves his knees behind him. The ultimate result is that he will learn to evade the rider's directions, drop behind the rider, chip in at the jump, and will probably refuse to jump the fence altogether in the end.

Your correction as rider should be to close your leg and push him into the bridle. Also press your whole body weight into your heels (pressing your heels down and back), instead of allowing your

The reins are all that are holding the rider on. If they broke, she would fall over his tail. She needs to practice her crest release.

ABOVE: *The rider is ahead of her horse and has lost control of the situation. Her loose lower leg has slid back as she grips with her knee only.* BELOW: *The rider is just a little ahead of her horse and could be resting her hands more solidly on the crest of his neck.*

ABOVE: *The rider is looking down, and as a result her body has collapsed on the horse's neck.* BELOW: *The rider is ducking badly to the left. She has made a good jumper into a dangerous knee-hanger.*

upper body to flop on the horse's neck. Then, over low simple jumps, practice grabbing the mane and holding yourself in a half seat over the top of the jump. Once that is mastered, you can practice a crest release, resting the hands partway up the mane.

Habitual dropping of the eyes over the top of the jump is another cause of upper-body difficulties. As a result your body will collapse on the horse and force his front end down. To correct this fault, you should practice looking at a predetermined point on the far side of the jump as soon as you have seen your distance to the jump.

Ducking to the left or right when the horse is in the air is a habit that goes along with dropped eyes and often is corrected with the same exercise as for that fault. Ducking puts the horse off balance and affects his jumping form.

Another common fault occurs when you drop back too quickly while the horse is in the air or just landing. This fault discourages the horse from rounding his back over the jump. The first correction is to check the lower leg position constantly—press the heel down and in, keeping a snug lower leg. Holding the half seat at all gaits strengthens the supporting lower leg. It is also helpful to practice over a lot of low jumps, holding yourself in the proper position by

The rider is supporting herself on the horse's mouth and preventing him from getting round over the jump.

ABOVE: *The rider is over her hands. The reins are too long and she is still hanging him in the mouth.* BELOW: *The rider has opened her fingers, a common and minor fault. One day, however, she may lose her reins or break her fingers.*

grasping a piece of mane before the takeoff and holding the mane until a stride or two after landing.

The very low dropped hand is a less common fault nowadays, because so many riders are taught the crest release. A very low hand often leads to a collapsed upper body over the top of the fence. Such a rider should practice resting the hands up on the crest of the horse's neck over many low jumps.

In short, by concentrating on the deep heel and strong leg, looking ahead, and resting the hands on the neck, you can correct most common riding faults that occur once the horse has left the ground.

The Horse: Some Common Jumping Problems

Whenever you have difficulties with your horse, your first question should always be, Is he hurting? Is he sore? Once you have ruled out any physical difficulties, address yourself to the horse's mental state.

The rider is landing just right here, though her lower leg could be wrapped around the horse a little more to support her better. This jump is fine, but were it bigger she might fall back a little without that lower leg support.

Is he frightened? Was he overfaced yesterday? Or, Has he been drilled too much lately? Does he need a couple of days off? Or, Has he had too much time off lately? Have I been too lax and lenient? If the horse is not sore and not overtrained, you have to figure out the best way to correct the specific problem. Most corrections are achieved by doing the opposite of what the horse wants to do. If he rushes, make him wait. If he hangs back, make him go forward. If he runs out to the right, turn him to the left, and so forth.

A horse can only perform to the limit of his talent. The rider as trainer should avoid as much as possible asking the horse to do what he simply is not physically and mentally capable of doing. If a 4-foot course is a struggle for him, sell him to a junior or amateur rider who only wants to jump 3 feet 6 inches. I have seen more than one game, good-jumping, large pony pushed beyond his capacity to do Medal and Maclay courses and ruined as a result. In order to save his skin, he becomes first a cheater and finally a stopper.

If a horse is short-strided and/or a short jumper, the rider should

The rider is jumping out of hand, maintaining contact with the horse's mouth in the air—not for novice riders, but for advanced riders with perfect control of their bodies.

help him by making sure that he has plenty of pace, by lengthening the horse's stride, and by moving up early in his lines. For example, a normal 12-foot-stride distance, about 72 feet, will ride long for a short-strided horse. So to do the five strides comfortably, the rider should press the horse forward with his legs upon landing from the first fence of the line. This kind of a horse is more comfortable leaving from medium spots, so keep his engine well revved and don't look for huge, long distances.

A cheater is different from a short jumper. Usually a cheater is sore or scared. Instead of leaving from a nice spot at a jump, he chops in an extra stride and pops it. One correction is to get the cheater closer to the jump by an increase; in other words, ride him forward to a deep spot instead of asking for a long takeoff. Reinforce the takeoff with a stick as needed.

A stopper always should be punished. A refusal to jump a fence, for whatever reason, is a serious disobedience and must be treated as such. After a refusal, a horse should be made to face the jump and should get at least one good crack with the stick. Of course, as I said earlier, the degree of punishment varies with the particular situation. If a horse is a habitual stopper, you should contrive situations that invite him to stop and then punish him severely. One method is to approach the jump with very little urging; another is to make him jump a course with little or no warmup first.

A rusher will sometimes hurry to the jump as soon as he sights in on it, then stop. Your correction is to punish the stop and then regulate the rush by circling and even pulling up the horse at the jump.

Rushing to the jumps is one of the most common riding problems; horse and/or rider become anxious and hurry toward the fence. The best cure for anticipation is lots of slow work. Walking or trotting low jumps right to the point of takeoff is an excellent exercise. If the horse becomes anxious, then make the jump lower until he can do the exercise calmly and correctly. Correct execution of the most simple exercises is the only real foundation for more sophisticated work later on.

Circling in front of the jump is another exercise that discourages anticipation. You must be sure not to communicate when you intend to jump by getting anxious yourself. A good, quick cure for anticipation is pulling up in front of the fence; this also teaches the horse obedience to the rider's aids. In other words, if you have months to

The rider is in the air for the next fence. Often this is necessary in a timed jump off in a jumper class, but it is an unnecessary mannerism in the equitation division.

correct the rusher, the low jump and circling method is preferable; but if you have only a few days or a few minutes to prepare for something important, then the pull-up method is more effective.

With a confirmed rusher, the rider may have to circle or pull up ten, twelve or even twenty times before the horse relaxes and approaches the fence calmly. Circling or pulling up does not teach a horse to stop; rather, it teaches him to wait for direction from the rider. The only danger of pulling up and circling is that you may use these exercises incorrectly; you may pull up or circle when you can't find a distance that suits you. In this situation, pulling up and circling can create very serious riding problems; you will find that you are using the pull-up as an evasion, not as a teaching device. Riders who work a lot on their own without a trainer's supervision often get in the habit of pulling up instead of working out a distance problem.

In contrast, a horse that is reluctant to leave the ground, or a horse that dwells in the air, needs a cluck and a stick to press him forward as he takes off. Otherwise, sooner or later he will land in the middle of a jump and scare himself.

A runout at a fence is a different kind of evasion. Often, a horse that runs out to one side or another of the fence has been bulging out or cutting in on his turns; in other words, you do not have control of the horse on the approach to the fence. To prevent runouts, you should be sure that you ride straight toward the middle of the fence, thereby discouraging any lateral evasion. A runout is essentially a

Use of a draft rail on the landing side of the jump to keep the horse out of his left corner. Rider is sitting well .

refusal and should be punished in the same way. The rider should place extra emphasis on keeping the horse straight.

Another lateral evasion occurs when a horse drifts to one corner or the other after takeoff. Very often, he drifts because he is sore and is trying to save himself. (For instance, if a horse is sore on his left front leg, he will drift to the right corner of the jump.) Here again, you must first rule out possible physical causes. Some horses learn to drift because their riders are sloppy and do not insist on their staying straight. To correct a drift, the rider should carry his stick on the side to which the horse drifts, and upon landing, he should turn the horse immediately toward the opposite direction. Placing rails on the ground perpendicular to the fence also discourages the drifter, as does

Schooling over a fence with the ground rails rolled out to encourage the horse to jump rounder. The rider is just right here.

jumping him over sharply crossed rails. However, the best prevention is to insist on straightness throughout.

Some jumping problems are really style variations that can be ridden out to some extent. (I advise you not to buy a horse with really serious style problems, however.) Horses with style difficulties need constant reminders to get them to hold their form. For example, a horse that is on his forehand, or that is slow with, or hangs, his knees will do better if ridden with a shorter, livelier stride, arriving long and balanced up at the jump. Such style problems can be improved somewhat with an accurate, intelligent ride. However, if a horse does hang his knees, he will always do so to a greater or lesser extent depending on his training. Rolling rails 3 to 4 feet away from the jump on both sides will help him, as will a step oxer (an oxer with the back rail higher than the front rail). Horses that twist or tilt in the air sometimes stay straighter if the rider counteracts the twist or tilt with his weight.

Most difficulties arise because the horse has not been ridden properly; he has been allowed to become sloppy and disobedient on the flat. Horses do not maintain their level of training by themselves. Their improvement or deterioration depends solely on their riders and trainers.

8

Preparing for the Horse Show

In many ways a horse show is analogous to a test or examination in school. You are testing yourself and your horse to see if you have both been doing your homework properly. Last-minute sprucing up (or cramming) is no substitute for good, consistent day-to-day attention to details. The horse needs proper feeding and care every day if he is to be in top physical condition when you show him. (For guidance on how to condition your horse and how to turn him out properly at the horse show, I recommend the book *Grooming to Win,* by Susan Harris. Study it carefully if you are at all serious about riding and showing.) Riding your horse, you see, is only part of your job; there are countless details that have to be attended to in order to present a good performance in the ring.

Your horse's mental preparation is just as important as his physi-

SUE MAYNARD

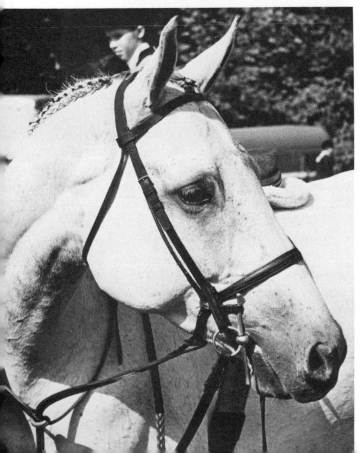

A bath, a trim, and a good braid job can transform a nag into a beautiful show horse.

cal conditioning, and your training program should take both into consideration. For instance, don't coast along for weeks and then decide one or two days before the show to teach him something brand new, like flying changes or the counter canter. The last few weeks before the show should be a review of what your horse already has been taught, with emphasis on his weak points, not just on what he does well.

Professional advice as to what shows and what classes you should enter can be of great help. As a general rule, if you are on your own you should start with very easy classes, possibly just flat classes at the first couple of shows. Get to a show early and school your horse over some of the jumps before the show starts. If your horse schools well in the morning, and if the courses are simple, straightforward, and inviting, then you may decide to show over jumps as well.

The results of your first endeavors will tell you how to proceed. (By "results" I do not mean necessarily the ribbons and trophies you may or may not win. Anyone who becomes more preoccupied with winning ribbons than with improving himself and his horse is headed in the wrong direction and ultimately will not achieve much.) Assume, for instance, that you showed in a novice equitation, hunter, or jumper class. (Novice classes are open to horses or riders who have not won three blue ribbons in their respective division; limit classes, to those who have not won six ribbons, and so forth.) A limit class is coming up. If you got around nicely in the novice class, you may want to do the limit, where the course will be slightly more demanding. On the other hand, if you felt the novice was enough, you may do better to leave it at that. When you are faced with decisions like this, professional guidance can be a big help. Often, just having someone there to say "Go on, you can do it" will give you that extra boost of confidence to do it—and do it well. If you get in a little mess, seek help. Get an accomplished rider to show the horse in a class or two to restore his confidence.

The Formal School

If the horse and rider have not shown recently, that is, some time within a week of the coming horse show, they should have at least one fairly formal school over a course of the sort the rider expects to jump at the show. The jumps should be about the height and width of the jumps expected there. If the rider has studied the ques-

Hans Richter, Age ten, on his Gwynedd Ask Me. This pony has left the ground from rather a long spot and is really "flying" the jump. He is a wise old man, having taught at least eight children to ride, many of whom have gone on to brilliant riding careers. Here he has "taken over" as he is apt to do when he sees his spot before his rider does. He knows to gather himself when he lands, and if his rider starts looking for bigger and bigger spots, he is smart enough to wait it out until he sees what he considers a good safe spot.

tions raised by the course designer at previous shows, he will be better able to prepare himself by setting up similar lines, turns, and combinations at home. Also, the schooling ring at home should be made to look as much as possible like the ring or outside course at the forthcoming show. For instance, in the fall, when the indoor shows are coming up, my ring at home is cluttered with all kinds of jumps, especially lots of little narrow jumps. There are many fences off of short turns, as featured in indoor rings. Difficult lines, verging on the impossible, are everywhere. The courses for the Medal and Maclay finals historically are not simple and straightforward.

A formal school is characterized by a short, snappy warmup on the flat and over a few schooling fences to simulate show conditions. (Before the National every year we practice warming up in a schooling area smaller than the one in Madison Square Garden—smaller even than my living room. This rehearsal prepares horses and riders so that they are able to warm up properly despite the cramped schooling conditions at that show.)

After a brief warmup, the rider proceeds around the course. For an intermediate or better rider on a made horse, my favorite first fence for a formal school is a simple looking but slightly wide oxer; riders who are careless about getting their pace before starting are quickly made aware of their error.

As the horse proceeds around the course, pay particular attention to his ridability. Whenever schooling, you should go against the problem, not with it. If a horse lands on the wrong lead and misses a change at the corner, circle and get it right. Circle again to settle him, if necessary, before proceeding.

If the horse is fresh or fiddles on the turn, circle him until he settles. Circling is a better remedy for freshness than stopping and backing, which is usually too severe a correction. But if a horse is lugging and boring around the turn, then stopping and backing are definitely in order. I like to stop a lugger, even if he is just a little bit heavy.

Also on the turns, pay attention to possible lateral evasions—bulging out or cutting in. Again, circling is a good correction, with the rider firmly but tactfully keeping the horse balanced on the turn.

Usually my equitation riders jump the course a second time without stirrups, and we incorporate some flat tests in the course. For instance, the rider may want to trot a fence, or do some changes on a line, or a turn on the haunches. Sometimes the course has to be jumped several times to get a smooth, even performance. Here again, judgment comes into play, and a trainer or ground man can be of invaluable help. How much is enough? How much is too much? As Kathy Kusner has said, "Do enough but not too much." It is better to do too little rather than too much. Don't ever be afraid to sacrifice perfection in favor of the apparatus. Never risk breaking down your horse to achieve a goal in his training.

A Sample Schooling Course

This is a fairly straightforward hunter or equitation course for a formal school at home or at a horse show. It is suitable for a ring about 75 by 150 feet. The course asks a couple of significant questions. The first line is set on the 12-foot stride and will probably ride a bit forward in four or five strides, depending on whether the distance is 60 feet or 72 feet. With this kind of a situation, I tell my riders not to settle after the first fence, but to keep going until they see the distance to the second fence and are prepared to meet it just right. An override here is far better than an underride; you don't want to arrive long and weak at the second jump, which, according to the chart, is imposing.

After fence 2, hold the horse out and use the turn to look in at fence 3. Look first for the line from 3 to 4, then for your distance to fence 3. The distance between 3 and 4 measures shorter than between 1 and 2. It will definitely ride shorter for several additional reasons: (a) it is the second line of the course, not the first; (b) jumping the oxer into the line will carry your horse farther in—his arc will be bigger; (c) the second line is heading toward the in gate; (d) fence 4 is simple and inviting, he has seen it before and will not back off there. Here the course designer wants to know if you and your horse can shorten smoothly and fit the strides in neatly, or whether you will be late shortening, or whether he will be disobedient and not shorten and pop fence 4. So as you land over fence 3, you must shorten immediately to fit the correct number of strides in, again four or five, depending on whether the distance is 58 feet or 70 feet. A hunter rider may prefer to ride indirectly from 3 to 4, drifting out toward the rail to give his horse more room so he won't have to shorten the stride so much. A hunter round should look natural, not computerized—even though it is. I would advise the equitation rider to ride directly from 3 to 4 to show he understands about shortening and knows how to do it well. This sort of move distinguishes the polished rider from the unpolished rider, who may wander between fences 3 and 4 and arrive there right—just by luck.

The next question the course asks is whether you can maintain

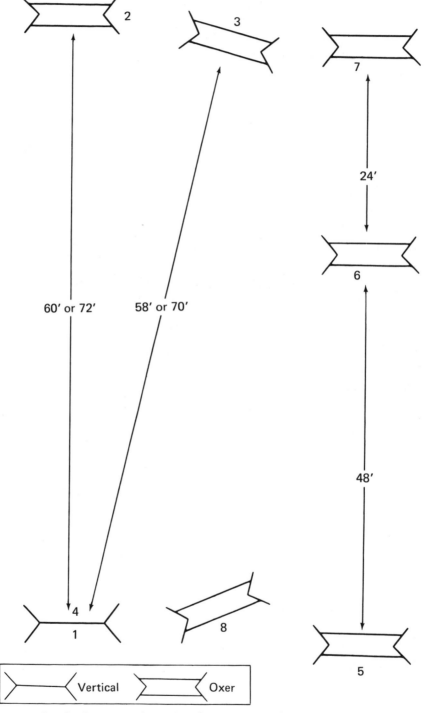

A sample schooling course for a ring about 75 to 100 feet.

the pace and impulsion past the in gate and ride aggressively down the next line. The three strides from 5 to 6 will ride forward; the oxer in-and-out may need an override, depending on the horse.

The final question of the course is the clincher: will your horse settle nicely around the turn and canter obediently down the whole length of the ring toward the out gate and jump the last fence kindly, or will he take over and drag you to or through the last jump? Another important question is being asked of the rider: if you've had a perfect trip, can you stay calm on that last canter and find a nice spot, or will you either rush or be too careful and conservative—and blow it?

The course should be modified for novice or very green horses. The first modification is to have the green horse skip fence 4. Make the in of the in-and-out a vertical and in general make that line as inviting as possible, possibly lowering fence 5 as well.

Schooling Versus Showing

When you are schooling your horse, you concentrate on his *weak points,* on trying to improve or, better yet, eliminate them. When you are showing your horse, you want to demonstrate his *good points* and hide his shortcomings as much as possible. A good competitive rider has a real knack for finessing the bad moments and making them seem as if everything is going fine. For example, sometimes even the most obedient horse will try to get strong and take over on a big, open outside course, especially going toward home. If you were schooling him, you'd circle him or pull him up. But when you're showing him, you have to cool it. Nothing can be gained by fighting him; that only tells the judge your horse is getting strong. On the other hand, you can't just let him go; that is too dangerous. So, tactfully, you have to persuade the horse to listen to you.

During the course of a show, you will have opportunities to school your horse, and you should take advantage of those opportunities. If a mistake early in your round puts you out of the ribbons, use the rest of your round as a schooling exercise. If your horse is slow off the ground, use your stick on the takeoff. If he is hurried, let him get a little deep to a couple of jumps and hit them, so that in the next class he will be inclined to back off. Our top Grand Prix riders use the less important classes as schooling rounds so they will be sharper for the big classes.

The Final Schooling

If your horse is showing in the equitation and the hunter divisions, he should not be too fresh. He should be longed and ridden on the flat until he is very quiet and obedient. Never mindlessly jump your horse back and forth over fences to work him down; it only teaches fresh horses to be rushers, and no horse's legs need that kind of pounding.

Most horses brighten up in the ring, so be sure yours is worked down enough. It is maddening to lose classes just because the horse is too fresh and won't listen, or bucks on the turns. Even normally placid horses can become silly due to changes in the weather, so if cold weather is expected, allow plenty of time for working your horse down the day before and again the morning of the show.

A horse showing in the jumper division does not need to be worked down as much as the hunter or equitation horse. He is more likely to jump clean if he is somewhat bright. However, he should not be so fresh he is easily distracted and does not pay attention to his work.

Be sure to longe or work your green horse thoroughly before taking him to the show. If he arrives at the show fresh, all the excitement will really set him off. Green horses need plenty of opportunity to get familiar with the show grounds. In the case of a one-day show held nearby, take your green horse over to the show grounds a day or two before the show and ride him around. Actually, it is a good idea to take green horses to a couple of shows just to school them there and accustom them to all the activity. This is especially good for horses off the race track, who tend to be quite nervous and excited at their first few shows. There really is no point in showing them until they are able to pay attention. Even if the show does not permit schooling in the ring or on the outside course, at least work on the flat and hop over some jumps in the schooling area. Work, as I have said, on the horse's weak points; don't just practice the things he does well in order to impress the bystanders. If any major disciplining is necessary, however, avoid doing it in public; try to take care of it in the privacy of your own ring before you go to the show.

If the schooling area is the only place at the show where you can jump, be inventive with the equipment that is available. Make some kind of a pattern out of the individual jumps. If possible, set up a vertical-to-oxer gymnastic and work the hunter or equitation horse

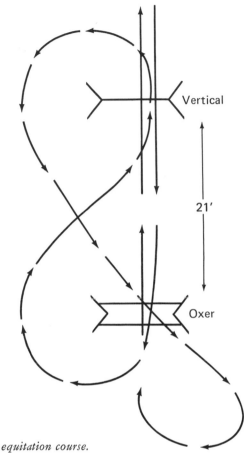

Vertical

21'

Oxer

An improvised equitation course.

back and forth over it. The distance should be approximately 21 to 22 feet for fences 3 feet 6 inches and under. Jump individually across the vertical and then the oxer. You can even make up a little equitation course (see diagram). For the jumper, build the combination higher and wider, and lengthen the distance to 24 to 25 feet, or make a Swedish (X) oxer. Obviously, if other riders are schooling at the same time, the course cannot be so elaborate. The jumps do not have to be jumped together, but try to place them so that the distances are related. Jumpers usually have to be schooled over a few higher jumps to raise their sights for the show.

Don't be intimidated by people who try to monopolize the schooling area; you have as much right to use the jumps as they do. By the same token, don't monopolize the jumps yourself; such behavior is annoying to the other exhibitors.

Schooling in the Ring

Many of the smaller shows permit schooling in the ring before the show starts. This is especially helpful for spooky horses and green horses, who go much better in a show if they get a feel of the ring and the jumps beforehand. A very green horse is likelier to hop over a spooky looking jump with equanimity if he is allowed to sniff it first, than if he is beaten over it by his rider the first time or two. On the other hand, for every honestly frightened green horse there are dozens of spoiled brats who have to inspect every fence before jumping it. Unless a horse is very green, I don't think he should be allowed to look at each fence closely before jumping it. Again, a rider with good judgment will know when to let the horse look over a strange jump and when to make him jump it straightaway.

During the schooling session, you should first make sure the horse is supple and obedient on the flat. Then you should trot some simple low jumps, then gradually work in the more difficult lines and turns. Equitation riders should check the day's courses if they have been posted and practice any offbeat lines; this gives a feel of the line before it is ridden in the class. Whether the courses are posted or not, the equitation rider should be inventive in his schooling and do as many different lines as possible and practice angling fences, pulling up, and trotting fences as well.

However, if the ground is hard, if the weather is hot, or if the horse is entered in a lot of classes, you must be careful not to overdo the schooling. If the ring is very crowded during the schooling time, you may want to just hop a few jumps and leave. Some horses just can't take all that commotion. Do enough so that the horse is properly prepared, but not so much that the horse becomes tired or, worse yet, goes lame because of overzealous schooling. I firmly believe that for every fence a horse jumps there is one less jump in him at the end of his career. Lydia Theurkauf, one of my riders, usually had her two horses very well prepared for their classes, but she never jumped one more fence than was necessary. As a result her horses are still showing successfully at the A shows, even though they are both now well into their teens.

Schooling in Indoor Rings

Whenever you school in an indoor ring, and especially if you are schooling in a strange indoor ring before the show starts, your primary concern should be to get your horse going forward and into the corners of the ring. Horses tend to back off indoors, so be aggressive and use a strong indirect inside rein and a strong inside leg to press him out into the corners. When schooling, exaggerate your turns, insist that the horse go into the corners much more than you plan to in the class. Then later, during the show, you will have much less difficulty with cutting in on the turn.

Schooling over the Outside Course

Many riders today do not have the opportunity at home to gallop around an outside course, to school in an open field over jumps where the distances are mostly unrelated. Even if jumps in open fields are available, outside courses often are neglected in working at home. This is because most show hunters are Thoroughbred horses bred for running, and many are revamped race horses with lots of memories of galloping fast down wide, inviting race tracks. Hence these horses don't need fast work over jumps; they do need slow work at home over cavalletti, gymnastics, lots of turns and practice at trotting fences. Now, at the horse show, the trick is to let yourself and the horse get comfortable with a hunter pace on an outside course without "blowing the horse's mind," as my riders say.

Schooling over the outside course, whether the day before or the morning of the show, should include plenty of slow work to start with. First trot some lowered jumps, then canter them individually, incorporating the usual flatwork between the jumps to keep the horse relaxed and obedient. If the horse drifts to the left or right, then circle him in the opposite direction from the drift after landing over each individual jump. Try to get a feel of the pace and the rhythm, a feel of the gallop. Next do sections of the course; put a few of the individual jumps together. Then do the whole course, being careful to gather the horse after each jump so that his frame does not get too long and strung out. Outside courses tempt the rider to look for bigger and bigger distances as the horse's stride opens. For one of my riders, the solution to this difficulty is to remind herself often "to gather and keep going." Both the "gather" and the "keep going" are important for a smooth and fluid trip around the course.

After schooling around the whole course, the horse may need to trot a jump or two, or the rider may even pull up in front of a couple of jumps to remind the horse to wait and to keep him from getting too eager later in the class.

9

Showing Your Horse

In flat classes, whether the rider or the horse is being judged, the routine is as follows. Unless the class is very large, the judge works all the participants as a group at the walk, trot, and canter. Martingales are not permitted in flat classes. Because many horses are one-sided and many riders are one-sided in position and influence on the horse, the judge must work them at all gaits in both directions of the ring.

Remember that you are expected to *show* your horse; you have to be seen in order to be judged. Often a judge will spend most of the time watching a class on one side of the ring; it is crucial that you make as many good passes by the judge as you can. This takes a lot of arranging. You have to watch the horses in front of you and behind you and, as you come around the turn, figure whether to cut in

*Ellen Raidt on Miss Jennifer Hines' Vibration (*ABOVE*) and Mr. and Mrs. John Kingery's Mr. Bar Do Too (*BELOW*). A top rider must be very versatile. Every horse has a different personality and different idiosyncracies. Also, showing hunters is quite different from showing jumpers, as illustrated by Ellen in these two pictures. The expression on her face tells the whole story: stillness and softness on the hunter, Vibration, contrasted with aggressiveness and determination to get to the other side of that big wide oxer clean on Mr. Bar Do Too.*

or drift out in order to get a good spot by yourself—alone in front of the judge. To quote George Morris in *Hunt Seat Equitation:* "The rider must keep three eyes open—one on himself, one on the other horses in the class, and one on the judge."

Hunter Under-Saddle Classes

In under-saddle classes, the horse is being judged. The rule book of the American Horse Shows Association requires "light contact with the horse's mouth." The horse should be obedient, alert, and responsive, and he should move freely. The judge is looking for the well-balanced horse who covers the ground with a long, sweeping stride. Some horses are better movers at the trot than at the canter, and vice versa. If your horse trots better than he canters, show him off at the trot, make good passes by the judge, and hide a little at the canter. Except in Green Hunter classes, the judge will ask eight horses at a time to hand gallop. Often a horse will take the opportunity at the hand gallop to buck and play. To prevent this let him gallop out at the turns and settle him going into the turns: ask for as much gallop as you can without having him blow up.

Hunt Seat Equitation Classes on the Flat

The hunt seat equitation judge will be examining the competitor's basic position—his seat, legs, and hands—and his control over the horse. He is not looking for the perfectly posed pretty position. He is also judging the rider's influence on the horse. He expects the equitation rider's horse to be well balanced and nicely bent on the turns. When you show in an equitation class, demonstrate that you know something about riding on the flat. Don't think only about your position. When the judge asks the class to reverse, don't just turn the horse around. Do a turn on the forehand or haunches.

Also, upon entering the ring before the judging actually starts, practice a few canter departs and/or the counter canter or any other movement on which you expect to be tested. You want to make sure your horse is prompt, and if the judge happens to be watching, you might catch his eye even before the class starts officially.

The class will, of course, first be worked as a group and then the judge may call for individual tests. Your response to his commands should be prompt but not rushed. Nervous or novice riders in competition are especially liable to pick up the wrong canter lead simply because they are in such a hurry that they neglect to balance their horses properly before striking off at the canter. So, whether working in the group or in the individual tests, be sure to take your time and get it right.

All the individual tests are listed in the AHSA rule book. (Most horse shows are members of the American Horse Shows Association and are governed by its rules. Participants in horse shows should become members and should learn the AHSA rules. For information, write the AHSA, 598 Madison Avenue, New York, NY 10022.)

The qualities desirable in the rider who shows in hunt seat equitation classes have been described as follows by George Morris, speaking at a clinic:

> He should have a certain *style* which incorporates sound basics but at the same time is personalized. His performance should be characterized by smoothness and precision. *Consistency,* always a great asset, has become a must quality in the brilliant rider. Another important consideration is the total picture, the combination of horse and rider together. There is also that indefinable quality—*theatricality*—which can be learned up to a point. Some riders seem to have a special flair for showmanship, a knack for being in the right place at the right time looking just right.

Classes over Jumps: Hunters, Hunt Seat Equitation, and Jumpers

Regardless of what division you are showing in, the class procedure over jumps is essentially the same. The competitors compete individually over a prescribed course that is posted at the collecting ring or at the in gate. At the major horse shows a jumping order is posted as well, and the entries must compete in the prescribed order. The order is rotated for each class in a particular division, so you must check your order each time well before the class begins.

Once you are at the in gate, the procedure is as follows. You walk or trot into the ring and make a circle about one third the size of the ring, picking up the canter about halfway around the circle. (If the time schedule is very crowded, the judge may specify a smaller area for your circle. If it is the first class or if your horse is green, you may want to take a little bigger tour of the ring.) You establish your pace and jump around the prescribed course, closing with a circle at the end.

SUE MAYNARD

Alex Dunaif on her Open Jumper Sudden Death. Alex is my most organized rider. She knows what shows she wants to do and plans the year's schedule accordingly. At the shows she always has all the necessary equipment in good working order. She makes sure she has plenty of time to study the course, knows when she is supposed to go in the jumping order, and has her horse properly warmed up and ready to walk in the ring when it is her turn.

Hunters are judged on performance, manners, and way of going. The judge is looking for smoothness and evenness throughout the course: over the fences, between the fences, and on the turns. If your horse lands on the wrong lead, he should change smoothly to the correct lead in the turn. As in the under-saddle classes, the judge is looking for a long, sweeping stride between the jumps ("the way of going") as well as a pretty picture over the top of the jumps ("style of jumping"). Hunters are expected to snatch their knees up and round their backs, making a pretty arc or bascule over the top of the jump.

Jumpers are scored rather than judged. Any rider who intends to show jumpers should study the Jumper section of the AHSA rule book, where the method of scoring is clearly defined.

Hunt Seat Equitation Classes over Fences

A hunt seat equitation judge must take into consideration both the rider's style and his or her performance in the class. In a recent

Mike Crooks riding Jackson. Mike has approached this water jump with just the right pace and impulsion. He found a good spot to leave the ground from and is letting Jackson jump it in beautiful form.

BOB FOSTER

AHSA-sponsored clinic for hunt seat equitation judges, Ronnie Mutch addressed himself very eloquently and appropriately, I thought, to the question of performance vis-à-vis style:

> A rider with exceptionally correct position may have a close jump or have all perfectly stylish jumps, but appear stiff or give the impression of all form and no feel. On the other hand, another rider may have some style faults, but he gets to all the jumps precisely and keeps his horse jumping softly, happily, and in good form. I would go with the latter, so long as his form faults were not too distracting. Often a rider will jump a fence in a perfect position, but for lack of balancing the horse properly on the approach, he causes it to hang its knees or come out of shape in some other way for which a hunter would be penalized.
>
> What I am saying is that regardless of how pretty the rider, he or she *must* get to all the spots.
>
> Naturally, I'm not advocating pinning the horse's performance in an equitation class. But I am cautioning against the emphasis being allowed to swing too far in either direction—style *or* execution. It is the good judge who can spot the riding weaknesses in the otherwise stylishly correct rider, and who recognizes the talent and empathy in the effective rider with a minor form fault.

Talent and empathy are important qualities that sometimes get overlooked because so much of our riding over courses has become very computerized. The distances between the jumps are clearly defined and in order to win one must ride them exactly to the inch. In our pursuit of accuracy and precision, discipline and obedience, we sometimes fail to recognize the soft, sympathetic rider.

Walking the Course

As an example of how to walk the course, refer to the schooling course on page 118 and assume that the distances have not been posted. Upon entering the ring to walk the course on foot, you would first plan your circle. In this case, a good plan would be to trot in past fence 1 and toward fence 3; get the canter near fence 3, establish your pace as you go by 6 and 5, maintain your pace around the turn, and then get on with it.

When you walk the distances between jumps, stand where you expect the horse to land and walk 3-foot strides (which you should measure and practice at home) toward the next fence, counting *1* 2 3 4, *2* 2 3 4, *3* 2 3 4, *4* 2 3 4, etc. Each four of your strides should equal 12 feet, or one horse's stride, so on *4* 2 3 4 you have counted four strides to the takeoff for the next jump. If you arrive at the takeoff to the next jump off stride, say, on 2 or 3, then you have to figure out whether to add a stride or leave it out. When there are options, the first person to show is at a disadvantage. He must analyze his horse's level of training and his stride as well as where the options occur on the course. On this particular course, the first line is right on the 12-foot stride and will ride forward since it is the first line. As you walk the turn, look for a landmark—a telephone pole or a particular post—something you can catch with your peripheral vision as a turning point while you are looking at the third fence. The distance from fence 3 to fence 4 will walk short and ride shorter for the following reasons: (a) the distance measures shorter on the tape; (b) the direction is toward the in gate, not away from it; (c) it is the second line on the course, not the first; (d) the third fence is an oxer and will carry the horse's arc farther out over the fence and consequently into the line; (e) the horse has already seen the fourth jump from the other direction and probably will not back off at it.

Notice on the next line how cluttered it looks as you walk toward it; and remember your horse may back off here, so you want to be there to support him with your leg. (An in-and-out away from the in gate usually demands an aggressive ride.)

Looking toward the last fence, notice how open and inviting that long run is, and remember to settle your horse before rounding the turn to the last jump. Here you will have to maintain an even pace and let a nice distance come up. Off a long turn, there is a tendency to rush a single jump like this or to be too conservative with it.

Upon landing, do a nice closing circle and trot or walk out of the ring. Remember, this is a horse *show*, so don't do excessive bendings and training as you exit on your hunter or equitation horse. On your jumper, you can bend and train all you want. The score, not the overall impression, is what counts in the jumper division.

Review your plan several times in your mind, and if possible watch a few horses go to get a better feel of the questions the course designer is asking. How forward is the first line? How steady the second? Try to watch at least one horse whose stride is similar to your horse's stride. (If you go third or fourth in the class, school before walking the course so you will have time to watch a couple go as well as jump a fence or two before your turn comes up.)

When you walk the course, look for incidental distractions—the lady with the umbrella at the in-and-out or the ferris wheel that might catch your horse's eye on the far turn. Also notice the footing. Is it deeper in some spots than others? That will make a significant difference to your horse. Is the footing in the ring different from that of the schooling area, and if so how will this affect your plan? Walking the course judiciously can be the equivalent of riding around it one time before you actually ride it. You owe it to yourself and your horse to know as much as possible about the course before riding into the ring.

Readiness

Horse shows are required to post the course at least one hour before the start of a class, so there is really no excuse for not knowing the course well in advance. Even so, who of us hasn't miscalculated at one time or another and arrived breathless at the in gate? In such a situation one must stay calm and get it together as well as possible. But don't make a habit of getting to the in gate in the nick of time. Even if the distances between the jumps are posted, you should watch as many horses as you can jump around in order to get an even better feel of the questions the course designer is asking. How steady *is* that "steady five," or how forward *is* that "forward four," or is that even six as even as it looked with the first horse? These questions can be answered best by watching closely. Also, in big, long classes things sometimes change as the class proceeds, and the person who watches only the first ten horses will not know that the even seven was done very smoothly in a forward six by nearly everyone in the second half of the class.

How long should one allow for warming up in the schooling area? Usually about ten horses is plenty of time; in other words, if you go twenty-fifth, get on when the fifteenth horse enters the ring. If the ring is small or the course is short, you may want to get on earlier; or if the ring is big and the course long, then ten horses may be too soon. Timing is of the essence, and good timing comes with practice. Being ready too early is always better than being late and feeling rushed. If you get ready too early, you can always jump a fence or two just before you go in. Some horses are better if they stand around a few minutes after schooling; others are better if they go directly from the schooling area to the ring. Remember, also, that some horses, especially old-timers who know what is coming, get anxious if they are made to stand at the in gate as horses go ahead

Tony Boxendale gives Katie Monahan a leg up on Johnny's Pocket. It takes a lot of teamwork to show a horse; good care in the barn is as important as a good ride in the ring.

SUE MAYNARD

of them. These horses are better off walking around within calling range than fretting in anticipation at the in gate.

About the Schooling Area

Usually the schooling area at the horse show includes at least three jumps: a cross-rail or low vertical for trotting, another vertical, and an oxer. The amount of time spent on preparations for a class depends on so many variables that it is almost impossible to generalize. Usually the warmup for the first class of the day or of the show is more extensive than warmups for later classes. Later in the day or the week, the schooling usually comes to the point more quickly.

Before every class, the horse should have at least a few minutes— and sometimes as long as twenty minutes—on the flat. First you should work on pace control: increases and decreases at all gaits, as well as some halts to review longitudinal obedience; then some shoulder-in, leg-yielding, and turns on the haunches to remind the horse about lateral obedience. As always in the schooling session, work on the areas where the horse is weak and work less on his strong points. I think it is important to avoid major clashes in the schooling area just before the class, since they tend to upset horse and rider both. Of course, occasionally these clashes are unavoidable, and appeasement in some situations serves no purpose at all.

The jumping phase of the warmup usually starts with a couple of trotting fences. It is important to have someone in the schooling area, preferably a ground man, who can advise the rider about the progress he is making, or if nothing else, set the jumps the way the rider wants them. Many "messes" in the schooling area occur because a rider simply jumps what is there instead of what his horse needs to jump.

For a green horse or a horse that backs off his first time in the ring, the schooling should be aimed at building confidence. Start with the trotting fence and if he is backing off, canter back and forth over the cross-rail to get him going forward. Then progress to cantering low verticals and eventually higher verticals with the rails rolled out 3 or 4 feet from the base of the fence. Next, the horse should jump an oxer, probably not a square oxer, but a step oxer (with the back rail higher than the front). Such an oxer builds confidence and scope. In the schooling area the horse should jump several fences at least as high as those he will encounter in the ring, perhaps even a little higher.

The horse that needs sharpening for one reason or another can jump an airy vertical or even a vertical with no ground lines at all. It also helps such a horse to jump oxers and fences that are con-siderably higher and wider than what he will encounter in the ring.

If possible, riders should also practice in the schooling area any specific or unusual lines and turns that will be presented by the course. For instance if the course calls for a sharp right turn to a jump, incorporate such a turn in the schooling, so it will not come as a surprise to the horse later on. Angling fences makes horses obedient and also gets them to snatch up their knees more quickly. Angling fences also makes the rider more definite and aggressive.

Reasonable facsimiles of odd jumps can be constructed for schooling. For instance, jumping a broken rail will prepare the horse to meet the narrow jump later in the ring with equanimity. A filled-in fence, such as an oxer with extra cross poles, also alerts the rider that he will have to ride more aggressively in the ring.

Jumping over a cooler draped on a fence in the schooling area is an excellent preparation for horse and rider before jumping a strange course in the ring. Spooky horses need to be pressed over anything strange looking, and most riders need to get a feeling in the schooling area of how the horse will back off in the ring. (On a windy day, wrap the cooler around the top rail instead of letting it flap menacingly in the breeze.)

A cooler spread on the ground serves as an introduction to a liverpool or other water jump in the ring. The cooler also can be spread on top of an oxer.

Before Entering the Ring

Before entering the ring, review the course one more time in your mind to be sure you have everything straight. You should have planned exactly where the circle will be, so when you enter the ring, you can be concentrating on how to start, not where.

Some horses need a jab with the spur or a couple of smacks with

Reviewing the course in her mind just before entering the ring.

SUE MAYNARD

the stick to wake them up and get them in the bridle before entering the ring. A big circle, if allowed by show management, is often a good idea in the first class to give the horse a feel of the ring. Trot close to any strange-looking jumps as you make your circles, but do not show them to the horse, since the penalty for that is elimination. Some horses fret if you wait in the ring for rails to be replaced or jumps to be reset; they are better off if you wait outside and then get on with the job decisively once you are in the ring. Never allow the horse's anxiety to make you feel rushed into starting too quickly. In fact, if you feel at all nervous or rushed, then take a little extra time walking in the ring before starting.

After the Class

After you have finished your round in a class, whether it was good, bad, or indifferent, try to analyze it objectively. Try to figure out what did work and why, as well as what did not work and why. Allow yourself to feel neither smug self-satisfaction nor abysmal despair; instead, be objective. Especially in the excitement of competition, an observant, objective ground man or trainer can save the day when an anxious rider thinks all is lost. Or, if you think you just had a fabulous trip, a ground man who noticed that your horse left a leg just a bit on the third jump will prevent your being horribly disappointed when the judge does not share your enthusiasm and call you back for a ribbon.

In short, after the class you have to figure out how to improve your performance the next time. And, as George Morris so aptly puts it, "the right way to do almost anything with horses is mainly a matter of using your natural intelligence in an uncomplicated manner." Plain old common sense is essential when you are training and showing horses.

A typical case in point is a young rider of mine who has a fairly fresh, forward-going, but very green pony that she keeps at home and trailers over once a week for a lesson. She is on her own a lot and needs to develop more common sense, as evidenced by her experience at their first indoor horse show. Her report from the show was that the pony didn't want to go forward, though at home the reverse is the case. To clarify the problem, we simplified it. If you were a little green pony all by yourself in a strange ring with strange jumps, what would *you* do? Certainly not get strong and hurry to

Nicole Busken, riding The Snow Goose. Together Nicole and "Richard," affectionately nicknamed after her father, had that elusive quality, theatricality. No matter how hot the day or how long the class, when Nicole and "Richard" walked in the ring, the judge sat up and noticed them.

the jumps, as you want to do in the familiar ring at home on a cold, windy day. And if you were the rider of that scared pony, what would *you* do? Sit still and do nothing, or be aggressive and ride forward, encouraging him in every way possible? Of course, the latter tactic is the one the girl adopted at the next horse show. Her aggressiveness gave the pony some confidence, and they got around the course quite nicely.

10

A Few Final Words

Probably the most important qualities you will develop through your involvement with horses are an enduring humility and an eagerness to learn. There is so much to learn and so many people and horses to learn from! Whatever the particular area of riding you are interested in, you will find much to be learned in the other disciplines. Possibly your main interest is in training for and competing in horse shows. That's fine, but at the same time never pass up an opportunity to gallop horse races, ride a dressage test, go fox hunting, play polo, ride cross-country, compete in three-day events, ride in point to points or hunter pace events or hunter trials. What you learn from the people and horses you encounter in related fields will some day have a bearing on what you are doing in your chosen specialty. Pay attention, too, to the various blacksmiths, veterinarians, hay men, and saddlers who cross your path. They have a way of dropping pearls of wisdom, so pay attention or you'll miss something important!

SUGGESTED READING

Anthony d'Ambrosio. *Schooling to Show.* New York: Viking, 1977.

Susan Harris. *Grooming to Win.* New York: Scribner, 1977.

Bengt Ljungkuist. *Practical Dressage Manual.* Richmond, Va.: Whittet and Shepperson, 1977.

George H. Morris. *Hunter Seat Equitation.* New York: Doubleday, 1971.

Jean Saint-Fort Paillard. *Understanding Equitation.* New York: Doubleday, 1974.

William Steinkraus. *Riding and Jumping.* New York: Doubleday, 1969.

M. A. Stonebridge. *A Horse of Your Own.* New York: Doubleday, 1968.

Gordon Wright and Michael Kelley. *Riding Instructor's Manual.* New York: Doubleday, 1975.

The American Horse Shows Association Rule Book. (Issued annually)
    American Horse Shows Association
    598 Madison Avenue
    New York, New York 10022
The Chronicle of the Horse (Issued weekly)
    P.O. Box 46
    Middleburg, Virginia 22117
Practical Horseman (Issued monthly)
    225 South Church Street
    West Chester, Pennsylvania 19380

INDEX

143